THE open kitchen

a fresh approach to cooking kosher

THE open kitchen

a fresh approach to cooking kosher

Published by SAR Academy
655 West 254th Street
Riverdale, NY 10471
openkitchencookbook.com

ISBN: 978-0-615-52472-6

1st Printing   2012   3,000 copies

W WIMMER
cookbooks
A CONSOLIDATED GRAPHICS COMPANY
wimmerco.com   800.548.2537

dedicated *in* memory *of*
Sheri Raskas z"l

"כשושנה בין החוחים כן רעיתי בין הבנות"
(שיר השירים ב:ב)

September 1, 1948 – February 27, 2009

welcome to the open kitchen

In late fall of 2009, a small committee of SAR community volunteers and hopeless "foodies" got together to help develop a concept for a new kind of kosher cookbook. Most of us were cooking enthusiasts who had grown accustomed to venturing beyond our own cookbook collections to find new recipes and meal ideas. The proliferation of food blogs, cooking programs, and non-kosher cookbooks had provided us with inspiring ideas that could easily be adapted for a kosher diet. What most of these alternative sources shared was simple — they all focused on using a wide variety of whole, minimally processed, and mostly fresh ingredients to achieve vibrant, flavorful dishes.

Our vision was to develop a collection of unique recipes that used a wide array of whole ingredients and that were relatively simple to make, beautiful to look at, and delicious to eat! After sharing this vision with friends and family, we were pleased to learn that there was a real interest in this kind of a cookbook.

We are thrilled to be able to welcome you to *The Open Kitchen — A Fresh Approach to Cooking Kosher.*

The Open Kitchen was lovingly developed and created by the members of the SAR community and was envisioned as a reflection of the values and spirit of SAR Academy and SAR High School. As SAR parents, we are blessed with the knowledge that, from the moment our children enter school each morning, it is not only their minds that are being nurtured and fed, but also their hearts, spirits, and imagination. It is our hope that *The Open Kitchen* will be as successful at providing its readers with a feast for every one of their senses.

We are honored to be able to dedicate *The Open Kitchen* to devoted SAR grandmother and community leader Sheri Raskas z"l. Sheri lived a life that exemplified the values and commitment to family and community that serve as the cornerstones of SAR Academy. These qualities were best expressed in frequent gatherings and meals she hosted at her home on Shabbat and during the holidays. Her grandchildren were often found in her kitchen, the center of the Raskas home, doing homework and just visiting while Sheri cooked or baked. Sheri was the consummate hostess, cook, and entertainer, exuding every aspect of Hachnasat Orchim. We could not have a more inspiring and worthy dedication for this special project. It is our hope that this book and the family moments its readers create will serve as a living honor to her memory and to the values of her life.

Food, at its heart, is all about family, love, sustenance, and sharing. Preparing meals should provide the home cook with as much joy as it does in those he or she is serving. It is our hope that *The Open Kitchen* provides you with that joy and inspiration when you cook your next family feast.

A quick note on how to use the book: Although the recipes have measurements and detailed instructions, they can easily be adapted to your own style and tastes. Many recipes include suggestions for variations that allow you to enjoy the dish in multiple ways. We encourage you to tweak, adapt, and experiment with the recipes as you see fit.

For the vision of *The Open Kitchen* to be realized, we ask you to make it your own. Betayavon & Enjoy!

The Editors, The Open Kitchen, 2011

about sar

SAR is a Modern Orthodox co-educational Jewish day school for nursery school through grade twelve, originally formed in 1969 through the merger of three Jewish day schools, Salanter Yeshiva, Akiba Hebrew Academy and the Riverdale Hebrew Day School. Located along the Hudson River in Riverdale, SAR has more than 1,400 students, and over 350 administrators, faculty, and staff, and is one of the largest yeshivot in the greater metropolitan New York area.

SAR is comprised of the Early Learning Center (nursery through kindergarten), SAR Academy (grades one through eight), and SAR High School (grades nine through twelve). The three schools combine to form a unique learning community dedicated to the belief that every child possesses a divine spark, has unique worth as an individual, and should be encouraged to achieve according to his or her own ability. SAR's warm environment promotes confidence, creativity, and enthusiasm for learning. In its approach to academics, SAR nurtures students to develop intellectual curiosity, critical thinking skills, and a lifelong love of learning and Torah. SAR has created a program committed to excellence in every aspect of its educational goals.

The magnificent architectural structures of SAR Academy, Jesselson Campus, and SAR High School, dedicated to the memory of JJ Greenberg z"l, were inspired by the visions of its dedicated and tireless educators, leaders and benefactors. The windows at SAR are important, both philosophically and experientially. Surrounded by this openness, and filled with light, SAR fosters and encourages reflection and inclusion. There is a powerful connection between learning, praying and the outside world.

Learning at SAR is "lived," coming alive in exciting and vibrant ways in the hands of caring and creative teachers. There is tremendous energy and enthusiasm for Jewish life and learning. Furthermore, the same holds true for the partnership between educators, lay leadership and the parent body. There is a unique sense of collaboration that characterizes these relationships; it is living educational life to the fullest.

The Open Kitchen, a project of the SAR Parent Teacher Council (SAR-PTC), was conceived, created and lovingly produced by the SAR community, including, parents, teachers, staff members, grandparents, alumni and friends. The SAR-PTC provides a way for parents to meet other parents, share their ideas, concerns, and experiences and simply get connected and know what is happening in school. PTC programs include social events and parenting lectures on childhood development, student success, parenting strategies, health and wellness, education and more. Parents can volunteer to share an area of expertise with a class or participate by organizing festive holiday celebrations.

The Open Kitchen was inspired by SAR and its "open" educational philosophy, providing a place where children are respected as individuals, taught to believe in themselves, and given the room they need to grow.

editorial committee

editor-in-chief
Shoshana Winter

executive editors
Yardaena Osband • Mona Freidin

founding editors
Tamar Benovitz • Aliza Major • Tami Bezborodko • Barbara Sopher

associate editors
Hindel Jesselson • Shimona Katz

copy editors
Rena Karol • Yonina Siegal

photography
Marc Matsumoto

food preparation and consulting
Patricia Clark Catering

online developer
Jeremy Horowitz

category editors

hors d'oeuvres *and* appetizers

Valerie Altmann
Talia Gollender
Ilana Milstein
Aliza Siegel
Toby Smith
Lilly Weisz

soups

Miriam Deutsch
Toby Smith
Vicki Turek

salads

Miriam Deutsch
Shani Reich
Vicki Turek

breads, grains, *and* pasta

Nava Cohen
Talia Gollender

vegetables

Danielle Fuchs
Liz Spevack

fish

Abby Glass
Lori Wolff

poultry

Amy Ciner Weisberger
Sandra Molinas-Sigal
Fagie Tager Wachsman

meat

Mitch Benus
Debbie Issacs
Lauryn Weiser

vegetarian entrées

Hindel Jesselson

desserts

Andrea Harris
Jennifer Kroll
Miriam Schachter

shabbat *and* holiday dishes

Tamar Benovitz
Deborah David
Julie Thomas

the planning committee

Valerie Altmann

Deena Berger

Nava Cohen

Sherry Cohen

Rivka Falk

Jennifer Fenster

Rita Feuerstein

Mona Freidin

Judy Friedman

Tova Gerson

Talia Gollender

Mendy Jesselson

Hindel Jesselson

Jennifer Kroll

Karen Kuflik

Lois Mandel

Ilana Milestein

Sandra Molinas-Sigal

Karen Raskas

Carrie Rose

Rena Rosen

Janet Rosenthal

Shoshana Shendelman

Aliza Siegel

Yonina Siegal

Edina Sultanik

Julie Thomas

Fagie Tager Wachsman

Lilly Weisz

Shoshana Winter

special thanks

Rabbi Binyamin Krauss

Debra May

Heidi Greenbaum

Rabbi Tully Harcsztark

Heidi Kane

Elisa Sastow

tasters, testers, hosts, and cooks

The Open Kitchen has been a culinary journey that began in the fall of 2009 with submissions of over 500 recipes, to the beautiful full-color cookbook you hold today. To help select our final recipes, we conducted a rigorous editorial and testing process that depended on the contributions of our amazing volunteers. We would like to thank all of the many hosts, cooks, and "tasters," who lent their time, homes, and palates to helping us select and perfect the recipes in *The Open Kitchen*.

Joanne Aranoff
Tamar Benovitz
Deena Berger
Rena Boniuk
Sarah Braum
Adina Burian
Michelle Burstein
Ilana Chill
Amy Ciner Weisberger
Aliza Haber Cohen
Debbie Cohen
Ruthie Craimer
Deborah David
Susan Dresdner
Margaret Danishefsky
Yael Edelstein
Rena Einzig
Tamar Eisenstat
Rivka Falk
Rikki Feuerstein
Rita Feuerstein
Zachary Feuerstein
Chaya Fine
Naomi Fischer

Dana Fishkin
Sharon Freudenstein
Mona Freidin
Daniella Fuchs
Tova Gerson
Abby Glass
Jennie Goldress
Atara Gorsetman
Nyla E. Greenbaum
Shari Hain
Jessica Haller
Andrea Harris
Shira Hammerman
Laurel Mayer Hecht
Ayala Helft
Sophia Hershman
Tami Bezborodko
Aviva Itzkowitz
Malky Jacobs
Dana Jason
Hindel Jesselson
Shimona Katz
Jennifer Kroll
Deborah Landesman

Alice Leibowitz
Lisa Levy
Rita Malek
Lois Mandel
Aliza Major
Steven Major
Elana Minkove
Dan Ordan
Elissa Shay Ordan
Yardaena Osband
Sherri Perlman
Abby Pitkowsky
Ari Raskas
Karen Raskas
Michael Raskas
Robyn Raskas
Shani Reich
Janet Rosenthal
Jennifer Saal
Michele Saks
Miriam Schachter
Beth Schwartz
Simone Semer
Shoshana Shendelman

Robin Shimoff
Lauren Mogul Shinar
Aliza Siegel
Yonina Siegal
Sandra Molinas-Sigal
Reva Slasky
Orit Smith
Toby Smith
Barbara Sopher
Susie Spievack
Edina Sultanik
Elana Tepler
Sara Susswein Tesler
Julie Thomas
Lizzie Parker Tropper
Fagie Tager Wachsman
Sandra Weinstein
Lilly Weisz
Tami Weitzman
Beth Willensky
Shoshana Winter
Laurie Wolff
Shira Wurzburger

recipe submitters

We were lucky enough to receive hundreds of amazing recipes from the immediate SAR community, including students, faculty, and parents, as well as many from all over the world, from friends, grandparents, alumni, and relatives eager to participate in the creation of the *The Open Kitchen*. We would like to thank everyone who took the time to share their special recipes with us.

Every recipe we received was reviewed by our editorial committee and tested numerous times by our tasting committee and their families. We received an overwhelming response of more than 500 recipes. Over 200 of these have been included in this book. We appreciate the enthusiasm of all those who have shared in this endeavor.

We have done our best to include every individual in our list of submitters who shared their recipes online, via email, and handwritten notes dropped at our offices. We apologize to anyone whom we might have overlooked. Every recipe we received helped to inspire the wonderful dishes in this book.

Michal Abehsera	Lee Botnik	Tamar Eisenstat	Jackie Gerson
Carmella Abraham	Sarah Braum	Nick & Kathy Fadda	Sylvia Genauer
Lavina Abraham	Nina Bruder	Ruth Fagen	Diana Gitig
Rachel Abrams	Debra Cohen	Rivka Falk	Janice Goldfein
Noelle Albanese-Levin	Judy Cohen	Sheila Feinerman	Jennie Goldress
Yiska Allerhand	June Cohen	Karen Fellner	Susan Goldstein
Anat Alperin	Nava Cohen	Jennifer Fenster	Talia Gollender
Elise Askenazi	Sherry Cohen	Rita Feuerstein	Paula Gottesman
Miriam Axelrod	Sharon Koren Cohen	Chaya Fine	Margot Kann
Edith Bayme	Margaret Danishefsky	Melanie Finkel	Francine Grauer
Shoshana Bender	Deborah David	Debbie Finkelstein	Jane Grauer
Deena Berger	Avi Deener	Marion Fishman	Barbara Green
Adena Berkowitz	Patrice Dweck	Taryn Fishman Bolnick	Linda Greenbaum
Linda Bernstein	Simone Dweck	Erin Fortgang	Blu Greenberg
Esther Bezborodko	Erica Edelman	Rose Frankel	Abbie Greenberg
Rivka Bezborodko	Julia Edelman	Mona Freidin	Halana Greenberg
Tami Bezborodko	Malka Edelman	Nancy Freifeld	Sandra Greenberg
Jessica Bienenfeld	Jennifer Eichenholz	Miriam Friedman	Michelle Greenberg-Kobrin
Devorah Bleiberg	Daphne Eidman	Daniella Fuchs	Rena Greenfield
Rena Boniuk	Chavie Eisenberg	Aviva Futter	Soo Greenfield

Susan Grobois
Jennifer Grosberg
Rachel Gutman
Susan Haber
Aliza Haber Cohen
Adina Hagege
Shari Hain
Jessica Haller
Andrea Harris
Laurel Hecht
Judy Hellman
Sophie Hershman
Kathe Hertzberg
Annie Hoffnung
Jennifer Ann Horowitz
Sandy Herman Horowitz
Ryan Hyman
Rachel Jacoby Rosenfield
Chana Jankovitz
Jesselson Family
Hindel Jesselson
Laurie Jesselson Lesnick
Haina Just-Michael
Heidi Kane
Shari Kanovsky
Judy Kelly
Joyce Kinches
Yaira Kobrin
Soosan Kohananoo
Patricia Koslowe
Dina Kramer
Jennifer Kroll

Talia Kupferman
Jay Kusnetz
Ilana Kustanowitz
Shulamit E. Kustanowitz
Jennifer Lavine
Alice Lebowitz
Beth Levine
Michelle Levine
Sharon Levine
Lisa Levy
Sharon Lewis
Sheryl Li
Emily Lichtman
Sheryl Littmann
Rachel Loonin
Tiki Lyons
Lea Malek
Rebecca Malek
Karen Mann
Malka Margolies
Judy Matthews
Eldar Mayouhas
Tova Mermelstein
Ilana Milstein
Sarah Zitter Milstein
Stephanie Minkove
Paulette Morris
Michele Morse
Nataly Neuwirth
Yardaena Osband
Joan Paru
Susan Polin

Susan Presby
Gary Pretsfelder
Karen Raskas
Robyn Raskas
Sarit Rayburn
Carrie Rose
Rhona Rose
Ayelet Rosen
Rena Rosen
Dina Rosenberg
Ezra Rosensaft
Janet Rosenthal
Michele Saks
Julia Salter
Seema Savin
Brenda Schachter
Miriam Schachter
Jill Schanzer
Esti Schloss
Beth Schwartz
Dylan Schwartz
Lindsay Setton
Paige Shaw
Elissa Shay Ordan
Shoshana Shendelman
Andrea Sherman
Lillian Sherrin
Yonina Siegal
Aliza Siegel
Laura Siegel Rabinowitz
Toby Smith
Barbara Sopher

Harriet Spevack
Liz Spevack
Ruthy Stavsky
Judy Stein
Sara Susswein-Tesler
Fagie Tager Wachsman
Sylvia Taubenfeld
Sharona Thall
Zippy Thall
Julie Thomas
Lynette Tulkoff
Shirley Wald
Elana Weinberger
Lilly Weisz
Audi Weitz
Beth Willensky
Chavie Wilner
Shoshana Winter
Goldie Witrock
Rebecca Wolf
Emily Yolkut
Rachel Yolkut
Tziona Zeffren
Michelle Zellner
Penina Zilberberg
Betsy Zimbalist

table of contents

notes

hors d'oeuvres *and* appetizers

hors d'oeuvres *and* appetizers

caponata

A savory and satisfying dip and a delicious topping for chicken or beef.

2   pounds eggplant (any variety)

1   tablespoon kosher salt

½   cup olive oil, divided

4   celery stalks, chopped

1   medium onion, finely chopped

1   can (4 ounce) tomato paste

2   tablespoons sugar

1   pound Italian plum tomatoes, seeded and chopped

10   large green or black pitted olives, roughly chopped

2   tablespoons capers (smallest), rinsed and drained

5   tablespoons white wine vinegar

     Black pepper, to taste

2-3 teaspoons chopped basil leaves

1. Cube eggplant and place in colander set over a bowl. Sprinkle with salt and set aside for 1 hour.

2. Heat ¼ cup of the oil in a large sauté pan over low heat. Add celery; cook for 15 minutes until softened. Add chopped onion and continue cooking until onion is soft and begins to change color. Remove vegetables with a slotted spoon and transfer to a bowl to cool. Add remaining ¼ cup oil to pan and increase heat to medium.

3. Rinse eggplant, shaking off excess water and add to pan. Cook for 10 minutes, stirring occasionally, until eggplant begins to brown and collapse.

4. Mix tomato paste with sugar. Add tomato paste along with chopped tomatoes, olives, capers, and vinegar to pan. Stir in cooked celery and onion. Season to taste with pepper. Reduce heat and simmer gently for 15 minutes or until mixture is thickened. Remove from heat and let cool.

5. Serve cold or at room temperature. Sprinkle basil leaves over caponata for garnish just prior to serving.

retro deviled eggs

PARVE

A 50's American classic that deserves a comeback.

¼ cup panko breadcrumbs

1 dozen hard-boiled eggs, peeled

2 teaspoons Dijon mustard

⅓ cup mayonnaise

¼ teaspoon turmeric

1 tablespoon grated shallot

½ teaspoon hot sauce

5 small cornichons or pickles, diced

   Salt and pepper

1 tablespoon paprika for garnish

1. Preheat oven to 350 degrees.

2. Bake panko crumbs on a rimmed sheet for about 10 minutes until lightly browned. Set aside to cool.

3. Slice eggs in half. For easier cutting, spray knife with cooking spray. Remove yolks and place in a large bowl. Set whites aside on a tray. Add mustard, mayonnaise, turmeric, shallots, hot sauce, and cornichons to yolks. Mash yolk mixture with a fork until smooth. Season yolk mixture with salt and pepper to taste.

4. Place egg white halves on a serving plate. Fill each egg white with a heaping teaspoon of yolk mixture. For a fancier presentation, use a pastry bag fitted with a star tip to pipe yolk mixture.

5. Just before serving, garnish each egg with a pinch of baked panko and dust with paprika.

guiltless guacamole

PARVE

Although guacamole is healthy, the fat can add up. In this version, creamy white beans are added to the avocado mixture, adding lots of volume without the extra fat.

1   can (15-19 ounce) white beans, drained and rinsed

1   tablespoon lime juice

1   ripe avocado

2   plum tomatoes

1   jalapeño pepper (seeds and membranes can be removed for less heat)

½   cup loosely packed cilantro leaves

¼   cup chopped Vidalia or Spanish onion

½   teaspoon salt

1. Purée beans and lime juice in a food processor until smooth. Transfer purée to a medium bowl.

2. Mash avocado into bean mixture and blend well with fork.

3. Cut tomatoes in half; remove seeds and chop.

4. In same food processor bowl pulse jalapeño, cilantro, onion, and salt until juicy and thick.

5. Stir tomatoes and jalapeño mixture into beans until well blended. Add additional lime juice and salt, to taste.

6. Guiltless guacamole is best used within several hours, but may be refrigerated overnight tightly covered.

green goddess dip *with* pita crisps

PARVE

The gorgeous color and fresh flavors of this dip will surprise you and your guests.

pita crisps:

½ teaspoon curry powder

5 tablespoons olive or vegetable oil, divided

6 pita breads, split open

dip:

1 shallot, finely chopped

½ teaspoon minced garlic

1 package (10 ounce) frozen peas, thawed

1 tablespoon chopped fresh mint

½ teaspoon salt

    Pepper, to taste

1. Preheat oven to 350 degrees. Combine curry powder and 2 tablespoons of the oil and brush mixture over inside of pita. Cut each half into wedges. Arrange pita oiled side up, on 2 cookie sheets. Bake 8-10 minutes, or until golden. Cool. May be made 1 or 2 days ahead. Store covered at room temperature.

2. Heat remaining oil in a small skillet. Add shallots and cook over medium-high heat about 5 minutes until golden and tender. Add garlic and cook 30 seconds more.

3. Purée cooked shallot mixture, along with peas, mint, salt, pepper, and remaining 3 tablespoons oil in food processor until smooth. Makes about 1⅓ cups.

4. Serve dip in bowl on platter and surround with pita crisps.

trio *of* mexican salsas

These variations on traditional red salsa are great with tortilla chips or as a relish for grilled burgers.

tomatillo salsa:

PARVE

1   tablespoon canola oil, plus additional for pan

2   fresh tomatillos

½   large Vidalia or Spanish onion

½   cup chopped fresh cilantro

3   tablespoons fresh lime juice

1   tablespoon sugar

2   jalapeño or serrano peppers, chopped, seeds and membranes removed

    Salt, to taste

1. Preheat broiler.

2. Oil a small baking dish.

3. Remove and discard papery skin from tomatillos. Cut tomatillos in half, place cut side down, and broil about 5 minutes until slightly blackened. Cool tomatillos for about 30 minutes.

4. Place all ingredients into a food processor and pulse until combined. Transfer to a bowl, cover, and chill in refrigerator for at least 1 hour.

mango salsa:

PARVE

4   champagne mangoes, peeled and diced

½   large red onion, diced

3   tablespoons finely chopped cilantro

4-5 tablespoons fresh lime juice

    Salt, to taste

1. Combine all ingredients and refrigerate for 3 hours before serving.

pico de gallo:

PARVE

1½ cups seeded, diced tomatoes

¼   cup diced red onion

1   teaspoon diced jalapeño

1   tablespoon minced garlic

    Juice of 2 limes

2   tablespoons cilantro, plus extra for garnish

    Salt and pepper

1. Combine ingredients in a bowl, seasoning to taste with salt and pepper.

2. Add additional jalapeño to increase heat. Best served the same day.

Note: Adjust liquid ingredients to your liking. The recipes above produce chunky salsas.

poached salmon salad with endive

DAIRY OR PARVE

Elegant and tasty — perfect for a cocktail party.

2   fresh salmon fillets (4 ounces each), skinned

1   small onion, finely chopped

1   scallion, green part, finely chopped

2   small stalks celery, finely chopped

1   bunch fresh dill, chopped

¼   cup mayonnaise

2   tablespoons sour cream, dairy or parve (optional)

1   tablespoon Dijon mustard

Juice of 1 lemon

Salt and pepper, to taste

2   heads endive

1. Bring 1 cup water to simmer in a large pot. Add salmon fillets in 1 layer. Cover and poach on medium heat about 7-10 minutes until salmon is cooked through, but still slightly pink. Remove filets from water with slotted spoon and set aside in a bowl to cool.

2. Gently flake salmon, keeping salmon chunky. Add onion, scallion, celery, and dill to salmon.

3. Mix remaining dressing ingredients in a separate bowl. Fold dressing into salmon mixture until evenly mixed.

4. Separate 8-10 leaves of endive. Put a scoop of salmon salad in each leaf.

5. Can be served either individually or on a platter.

stuffed figs *and* apricots

DAIRY

The unusual combination of flavors and textures makes these a sophisticated hors d'oeuvre.

10 fresh figs

5 fresh baby apricots

2 logs (8 ounce) goat cheese (either plain or flavored), sliced or cubed into 30 pieces

30 honey-roasted pecans

1. Preheat oven to 425 degrees.

2. Halve figs and apricots, place on a greased cookie sheet. Top each half with goat cheese and place 1 pecan in center.

3. Bake for 10 minutes until cheese is softened. Serve warm.

roasted spiced chickpeas

A tasty snack that's packed with protein.

3   cans (15 ounce) chickpeas

3   tablespoons olive oil

1½ teaspoons chili powder

¾   teaspoon garlic powder

1½ teaspoons cumin

¾   teaspoon powdered ginger

2   teaspoons kosher salt

¼   teaspoon black pepper

1. Preheat oven to 425 degrees.

2. Rinse and drain chickpeas.

3. Mix dry spices and set aside.

4. Toss chickpeas with olive oil and season with spice mixture. Transfer to a large rimmed baking sheet.

5. Bake for 45 minutes until browned and fragrant. Cool to room temperature.

6. May be refrigerated for several days.

chicken satay

MEAT

By threading the chicken through the skewers, they cook fast and stay juicy.

marinade:

⅓ cup molasses

⅓ cup red wine vinegar

5 tablespoons olive oil

2 tablespoons light brown sugar

2 teaspoons hot sauce

chicken:

3 pounds boneless, skinless chicken cutlets cut lengthwise into 1-inch-wide strips

Wooden skewers

1. Combine marinade ingredients in large bowl. Remove ¼ cup marinade and set aside. Place chicken in remaining marinade, cover, and place in refrigerator. Let marinate for at least 45 minutes to overnight.

2. Preheat oven to 425 degrees.

3. Remove chicken from marinade; thread onto skewers. Arrange skewers in a single layer on lightly greased baking sheet.

4. Bake chicken in middle of oven for 10 minutes. Flip skewers and baste with reserved marinade. Bake for an additional 5 minutes or until golden brown on both sides.

5. May be served with chili-lime or peanut dipping sauce from Summer Rolls (page 30).

mediterranean spiced mini turkey meatballs

MEAT

A great make-ahead finger food that is good even at room temperature.

1   small shallot, finely minced

2   tablespoons olive oil

1   teaspoon salt

1   pinch pepper

1   teaspoon coriander

1   teaspoon allspice

1   teaspoon cumin

1   pound ground turkey (white or dark)

1   egg

½   cup breadcrumbs

2-3 tablespoons canola oil

1. Preheat oven to 350 degrees.

2. Sauté shallot in 2 tablespoons olive oil until translucent. Add all spices and continue cooking for an additional minute. Set aside and cool.

3. Mix turkey with egg and breadcrumbs. Add shallot mixture, mixing well and form into miniature balls. Sauté in canola oil until browned.

4. Place meatballs on greased baking sheet. Bake for 10-12 minutes, or until cooked through.

5. Serve with your favorite dipping sauce.

summer rolls *with* chili lime *and* peanut dipping sauces

A gorgeous summer appetizer that is sure to impress.

4 ounces rice vermicelli

12 (5-inch) round rice paper wrappers, plus extra in case of breakage

½ red bell pepper, cut into 24 strips

½ yellow bell pepper, cut into 24 strips

½ Hass avocado, cut into 12 strips

½ (4-inch) seedless cucumber, peeled and cut into 12 strips

  Alfalfa sprouts

6 large basil leaves, thinly sliced

¼ cup cilantro leaves, coarsely chopped (optional)

6 mint leaves, thinly sliced (optional)

4 ounces extra-firm tofu, cut into 12 strips (variation)

1. Bring water to a boil in a medium saucepan. Stir in vermicelli and cook about 2-3 minutes until noodles have softened and are translucent. Drain noodles well and transfer to a bowl. Cool to room temperature, tossing occasionally to minimize sticking. Cut vermicelli with scissors into approximately 2-3-inch pieces.

2. Fill a pie plate with water. Working with 2 rice papers at a time, dip the papers in water, shake off any excess, transfer to a work surface, and let stand 30 seconds until softened.

3. Place a small handful of vermicelli on the lower third of each rice paper. Top with 2 strips each of red and yellow bell peppers, 1 strip each of avocado and cucumber, and a pinch of alfalfa sprouts. Top with a few strips of the basil and other herbs, if using.

4. Roll vegetables up in rice papers, folding in the sides as you go. Press gently to seal ends. Place finished roll on a clean plate.

5. Repeat with remaining rice papers and fillings. When all the rolls are made, cut in half on the diagonal and serve with either dipping sauce.

6. Sliced extra-firm tofu may be substituted for noodles.

chili lime dipping sauce:

2 tablespoons soy sauce

1 teaspoon sherry or brandy

2 tablespoons fresh lime juice

1 pinch chili powder

2½ tablespoons sugar

2 tablespoons water

1. In a small bowl, combine all ingredients; stir until sugar is dissolved.

2. Sauce may be prepared 1-2 days ahead.

3. Store in the refrigerator. Bring to room temperature before using.

Note: *Summer Rolls shown with tofu.*

peanut dipping sauce:

½   cup creamy peanut butter

1   tablespoon granulated sugar

2   tablespoons hoisin sauce

1   tablespoon soy sauce

1   small garlic clove, mashed to a paste

1   teaspoon Chile-garlic paste, hot sauce, or
      ¼ teaspoon hot pepper

1   tablespoon toasted sesame oil

     Juice of 1 lime

¼   cup water

1. In a bowl, combine ingredients and mix until smooth. If mixture is too thick, thin with additional water until desired consistency is reached.

2. Store covered in refrigerator for up to 1 week.

crispy polenta *with* mushroom ragoût

MEAT OR PARVE

In this recipe the polenta, or cornmeal, is cooked, chilled, and sautéed. It acts as the perfect bed for this earthy mushroom ragoût.

4   cups water

1   cup polenta

2   portobello mushrooms

10   ounces cremini mushrooms

6   ounces shiitake mushrooms, tough stems removed

1   tablespoon olive oil

1   small onion, finely chopped

1   teaspoon salt

½   teaspoon black pepper

2   sprigs fresh oregano

2   sprigs fresh thyme

¼   cup soy milk

¼   cup beef broth (¼ cup vegetable broth with 1 teaspoon soy sauce may be substituted)

2   tablespoons flour

2-3 tablespoons canola oil, for browning polenta

1. Bring water to a boil in a medium pan; add a pinch of salt to water. Slowly add polenta to boiling water, whisking briskly until incorporated. Continue cooking over medium heat for 3-5 minutes, stirring frequently until polenta is thick and cooked through.

2. Remove polenta from heat; pour mixture into a lightly oiled 9x13-inch pan. Cover with plastic wrap and refrigerate 2-3 hours or overnight, until set.

3. To prepare ragoût, lightly scrape gills from portobellos with a small spoon. Chop portobello, cremini, and shiitake mushrooms roughly and set aside.

4. Heat olive oil in sauté pan; cook onion until soft. Add mushrooms; continue cooking until mushrooms are soft. Season to taste with salt and pepper. Add oregano, thyme, soy milk, and broth. Simmer mixture uncovered until sauce has reduced and begun to thicken. Add flour slowly, stirring well to avoid lumps. Continue cooking 5-7 minutes until sauce thickens, stirring occasionally to prevent burning.

5. Remove polenta from refrigerator; cut into squares.

6. Heat canola oil in a large pan and brown polenta pieces on both sides until crispy.

7. Serve each polenta piece topped with a spoonful of mushroom ragoût. Garnish with fresh oregano or thyme.

"crab" cakes *with* rémoulade

PARVE

Imitation crab may be a new ingredient to some kosher cooks, but it's commonly used in California sushi rolls and has a delicate sweet flavor.

1 medium Vidalia onion, finely chopped

2-3 tablespoons olive oil

1 teaspoon salt

1 teaspoon pepper

½ red bell pepper

½ yellow bell pepper

2 stalks celery

½ teaspoon cumin

½ teaspoon smoked paprika

¼ teaspoon chili powder

1 package mock crab sticks

2 eggs

1 cup breadcrumbs

1 tablespoon Dijon mustard

¼ cup mayonnaise

Canola oil, for sautéing cakes

rémoulade:

½ cup mayonnaise

2 tablespoons pickle relish or 1 small pickle, chopped

1 green onion, finely chopped

2 tablespoons Dijon mustard

2 sprigs fresh dill, minced

1. Sauté onion in a pan with olive oil, salt, and pepper until translucent. Chop remaining vegetables and add to pan along with the remaining spices. Sauté vegetables until softened. Turn off heat and set aside to cool.

2. Remove crab sticks from package; roughly chop into a large mixing bowl. Add eggs, breadcrumbs, mustard, and mayonnaise. Fold in vegetable mixture.

3. With damp hands, form small cakes and place on a lightly oiled tray. Crab cakes may be covered and refrigerated several hours ahead. Heat oil in a large pan; sauté cakes until browned on both sides.

4. Combine rémoulade ingredients and refrigerate for 15 minutes or overnight to allow flavors to develop.

5. Serve crab cakes with rémoulade.

turkey siniyeh

MEAT

A Middle Eastern appetizer marrying the cool creaminess of hummus with the heartiness of warm mushrooms and turkey. A delicious and satisfying combination.

3 tablespoons extra virgin olive oil

1 medium onion, finely chopped

2 garlic cloves, minced

1 teaspoon salt

Pepper, to taste

1 teaspoon cumin

1 teaspoon turmeric

1 teaspoon paprika

10 ounces cremini mushrooms, trimmed and sliced

4-6 turkey breast cutlets, diced

¼ cup beef stock

2 cups hummus, store-bought or homemade (see recipe in Shabbat and Holiday, page 293)

1 bunch flat-leaf parsley, chopped

1. Heat olive oil in a large frying pan. Sauté onion, garlic, salt, pepper, cumin, turmeric, and paprika until onion is translucent. Add mushrooms and continue to sauté until mushrooms soften. Add oil if mixture is too dry.

2. Add turkey to pan; sauté until turkey begins to brown. Add broth and continue simmering 7-10 minutes until turkey is just cooked and all ingredients are incorporated. Make sure not to overcook or turkey will be dry. Remove turkey mixture from pan and set aside, pouring out any excess liquid.

3. To serve, spread hummus in the middle of a large serving platter. Add siniyeh around hummus.

4. Garnish with additional olive oil, paprika, and parsley.

thai beef lettuce cups

MEAT

The flavor profile of the beef is an exotic twist. The lettuce cup is a lighter version of a traditional wrap.

1	pound lean ground beef
1	tablespoon cooking oil
1	large onion, chopped
2	cloves fresh garlic, minced
1	tablespoon soy sauce
¼	cup hoisin sauce
1	tablespoon rice wine vinegar
¼-1	teaspoon Asian chili pepper sauce (optional)
1	can (8 ounce) water chestnuts, drained and finely chopped
1	bunch green onions, chopped
2	teaspoons Asian (dark) sesame oil
2	heads Boston lettuce, leaves separated

1. Brown ground beef in oil over high heat, stirring often until cooked through. Transfer beef to a bowl and set aside to cool.

2. Cook onion in the same pan, stirring frequently. Add garlic, soy sauce, hoisin sauce, vinegar, and chili pepper sauce (if using) to onion and stir. Add water chestnuts, green onions, and sesame oil; continue cooking about 2 minutes until onions are soft.

3. Combine mixture with beef.

4. To serve, spoon a portion of meat mixture into each lettuce leaf.

eggplant tempura *with* tomato basil salad

PARVE

An all-vegetable appetizer that will please a variety of palates.

eggplant tempura:

2 eggplants, peeled and sliced into rounds, medium thickness

   Kosher salt

   Canola oil for frying

2 eggs, beaten lightly

1 cup flavored breadcrumbs or panko crumbs

   Salt and pepper, to taste

salad:

3-4 vine ripe tomatoes, seeded and chopped

1 small onion, finely chopped

1 glove garlic, minced

1 small bunch basil, chopped

3-4 tablespoons olive oil

2 tablespoons balsamic vinegar

   Salt and pepper, to taste

1. To prepare eggplant, place eggplant rounds on a plate and sprinkle tops with kosher salt. Let rest for a few minutes until eggplant releases some moisture.

2. Heat oil in a frying pan.

3. Dip each eggplant round in beaten egg, then in breadcrumbs. Fry 3-4 minutes per side until outside is crispy. When done remove from pan; season to taste with salt and pepper.

4. To prepare salad, mix all salad ingredients and set aside to marinate at least 1 hour at room temperature.

5. To serve, place 2-3 eggplant rounds on a plate topped with tomato basil salad.

soups

beef stock

A hearty, flavorful stock.

4-6 pounds meaty beef bones

½-1 pound stew meat, cut into 2-inch chunks

Olive oil

1-2 medium onions, peeled and quartered

1-2 large carrots, cut into large chunks

1 large celery stalk, cut into chunks

2-3 cloves garlic, unpeeled

Handful of parsley, stems and leaves

1-2 bay leaves

10 peppercorns

1. Preheat oven to 400 degrees.

2. Toss stew meat, carrots, and onions with olive oil to coat. Add bones, and place in a shallow roasting pan.

3. Roast for about 45 minutes, turning bones and meat pieces after about 20 minutes. Continue cooking until nicely browned. Lower oven temperature if bones begin to burn. Remove pan from the oven when bones and meat are browned.

4. Place roasted meat and vegetables in a large (12-16 quart) stockpot.

5. Deglaze the roasting pan by placing it on the stovetop on medium heat (may cover 2 burners); pour ½-1 cup hot water into the pan. Using a metal spatula scrape up all of the browned bits stuck to the bottom of the pan. Pour browned bits along with water into the stockpot. Add celery, garlic, parsley, bay leaves, and peppercorns. Add cold water to the stockpot until bones are covered. Heat on high until almost boiling then reduce heat to low. Stock should be at a bare simmer. Cover the pot loosely and let simmer slowly for 3 and up to 8 hours.

6. Remove pot from heat. When cool enough to pour, strain stock. Discard bones and solids.

7. Let cool to room temperature then chill in the refrigerator. Any remaining fat will rise to the top and form a protective layer against bacteria while stock is in the refrigerator. If you plan to freeze stock, however, remove the fat before freezing.

chicken stock

MEAT

A tried and true recipe. Simple and delicious.

3 broiler chickens, cleaned and left whole

1 bunch leeks, washed and cut into large chunks

4 carrots, peeled and cut into large chunks

4-6 stalks celery, cut into large chunks

1 bunch parsley

1 tablespoon salt

12 peppercorns

1-2 bay leaves

12 cups water

1. Place chickens and water in a large stockpot and bring to a boil, skimming fat off top. Reduce heat to a simmer and add vegetables, herbs, and spices.

2. Cover pot loosely and simmer stock for 4 hours, skimming every 1-2 hours.

3. Remove stock from heat.

4. When cool enough to pour, strain stock.

5. Chill in refrigerator. Remove fat before using or freezing.

roasted vegetable stock

PARVE

Roasting vegetables first provides this stock with a deeper flavor profile. Can be used in place of a meat-based stock.

2-3 large carrots, scrubbed and cut into chunks

2 potatoes, scrubbed and cut into chunks

2 large onions, peeled and quartered

2 stalks celery, cut into chunks

1 sweet potato, peeled and cut into chunks

1-2 zucchini or summer squash, cut into chunks (optional)

½-1 cup green beans (optional)

1-2 ears of corn (optional)

2 large tomatoes, quartered

5 cloves garlic, unpeeled

3 tablespoons olive oil

1 teaspoon coarse salt

1 teaspoon pepper

¼ cup red wine or water

Handful of parsley, leaves and stems

Dill (optional)

4-5 sprigs fresh thyme (or 2 teaspoons dried)

2 bay leaves

2-3 tablespoons tamari or soy sauce

1. Preheat oven to 400 degrees.

2. Place all vegetables in a roasting pan. Toss with olive oil to coat. Sprinkle with the salt and pepper.

3. Roast vegetables in preheated oven 30-45 minutes until edges are browned. Transfer roasted vegetables and remaining ingredients, except soy sauce, to a large stockpot.

4. Place roasting pan on stovetop over medium-high heat. Deglaze pan with wine or water and transfer contents to pot (may cover 2 burners). If pan cannot be heated on a stove, simply add wine or hot water and scrape pan. Add enough water to pot to cover vegetables. Cover pot and bring to low boil. Partially remove lid and reduce heat to gentle simmer.

5. Add soy sauce and simmer for 45 minutes.

6. Taste stock; if bitter or too strong, add 1 tablespoon honey or dilute with water. Strain stock. Stock may be refrigerated 1-2 weeks or frozen.

authentic spanish gazpacho

Traditional Spanish gazpacho is a simple soup filled with bright fresh flavors.

1   (2-inch) piece crusty bread, crust discarded

2   cloves garlic

2   teaspoons salt

2   tablespoons sherry vinegar

1   teaspoon sugar

½   teaspoon ground cumin (optional)

2½ pounds ripe tomatoes, cored and quartered

½   cup extra-virgin olive oil

    Cubed avocado for garnish

1. Soak bread in ½ cup water for 1 minute. Remove from water and squeeze dry.

2. Mash garlic to a paste with salt.

3. Blend garlic paste, bread, vinegar, sugar, cumin, and half of the tomatoes in a food processor until tomatoes are very finely chopped. Add remaining tomatoes and process until finely chopped. With the motor running, gradually add oil in a slow stream, blending for about 1 minute.

4. Press soup through a fine mesh sieve into a bowl, pressing firmly on solids. Discard remaining solids. Transfer to a covered glass container and refrigerate about 3 hours until cold.

5. Season with salt and vinegar before serving.

6. Garnish with avocado cubes.

watermelon gazpacho

Watermelon is not just for dessert anymore.

5   cups diced seedless watermelon

1   small cucumber, peeled, seeded, and diced
       (about 1 cup)

1   medium-size red bell pepper, seeded and diced
       (about 1 cup)

1   medium-size yellow bell pepper, seeded and
       diced (about 1 cup)

1   small jalapeño pepper, seeded and minced
       (optional)

3   pale green inner celery stalks, diced
       (about ½ cup)

½   small red onion, diced (optional)

¼   cup finely chopped fresh mint

3   tablespoons fresh lime juice

2   tablespoons red wine vinegar

¼   teaspoon salt

1. Purée 4 cups of the watermelon in blender (or use immersion blender in a bowl) until smooth.

2. Mix in remaining 1 cup chopped watermelon and remaining ingredients; stir to combine.

3. Cover gazpacho and refrigerate 1-4 hours until cold.

4. Best when eaten the same day.

cremini mushroom soup

PARVE

An interesting twist on a traditional mushroom soup. The combination of vegetables and sherry adds new depth and flavor to this earthy soup.

2 pounds cremini or baby portobello mushrooms, chopped

2 onions, chopped

2 shallots, chopped

1 clove garlic, crushed

1 sweet potato, peeled and chopped

2-3 tablespoons vegetable oil

6 cups vegetable stock

2 tablespoons Worcestershire sauce

2 cups sherry

2 cups soy milk

Salt and pepper, to taste

1. Sauté mushrooms, onions, shallots, garlic, and sweet potato in vegetable oil until mushrooms are softened.

2. Place vegetable stock, Worcestershire sauce, sherry, and soy milk into a large pot.

3. Add sautéed vegetables to the liquid. Simmer gently for 1 hour.

4. For an extra smooth soup let cool slightly and purée solids with some liquid in a blender or food processor.

Variation: A heartier soup may be made in a crock pot with the addition of ½ cup barley. Sauté mushroom, onions, shallots, garlic, and sweet potato, as described above. Place vegetables, stock, Worcestershire sauce, sherry, and barley in a crock pot. Add 1 teaspoon each salt and pepper. Cook on low heat for at least 8 hours or overnight. Adjust seasoning. Stir in 1 cup soy milk before serving, if desired.

maple-roasted parsnip soup

Here parsnips are the star. This soup makes the most of their starchy texture and subtly sweet, fresh flavor.

1¼ pounds parsnip, peeled and sliced medium thick

3 large carrots, peeled and sliced medium thick

3-4 shallots, peeled and quartered

2 tablespoons olive oil

2 cloves garlic, peeled and finely chopped

2 teaspoons freshly chopped thyme

2 tablespoons maple syrup

1-2 quarts chicken or vegetable stock

Chives, chopped, and toasted pumpkin seeds, for garnish

Salt and pepper, to taste

1. Preheat oven to 400 degrees.

2. Place parsnips, carrots, and shallots on a large rimmed baking sheet.

3. Mix oil, garlic, thyme, and maple syrup in a small bowl. Pour maple syrup mixture over vegetables, tossing until evenly coated. Roast in preheated oven approximately 30 minutes until lightly browned and tender.

4. Set aside to cool slightly.

5. Place roasted vegetables in a large soup pot; add stock, salt, and pepper; cover and bring to a boil. Reduce heat and allow soup to simmer for 10-15 minutes. Transfer soup to blender or use an immersion blender to purée until smooth.

6. Garnish with chopped chives and toasted pumpkin seeds.

zuppa polpettini

A hearty meatball soup that can easily be a meal on its own.

1   egg, beaten

¼   cup breadcrumbs or matzo meal

1   pound lean ground meat

1   tablespoon plus ¼ cup chopped parsley, divided

½   teaspoon salt

Olive oil for frying

6-8 cups beef stock

6   plum tomatoes, peeled and roughly chopped

2   cloves garlic, minced

1   teaspoon dried oregano

1   cup uncooked orzo

1. Mix beaten egg and breadcrumbs or matzo meal into meat. Add 1 tablespoon of the parsley and salt to taste.

2. Form into mini meatballs and fry in heated olive oil until browned. Transfer meatballs to a plate.

3. In a stockpot, combine beef stock, tomatoes, remaining ¼ cup parsley, garlic, and oregano. Bring to a boil and reduce heat to simmer, partly covered, for 15 minutes.

4. Add orzo and meatballs. Cover and simmer about 10 minutes until orzo is cooked.

5. If desired, freeze before adding orzo. When reheating add orzo to cook.

roasted tomato soup

A late summer soup that makes the most of seasonal tomatoes.

24-26 plum tomatoes

Salt

1 clove garlic, finely minced

½ cup assortment of fresh herbs, chopped—
thyme, rosemary, sage, etc.

Olive oil, for drizzling

6-8 cups chicken stock or vegetable stock

1 tablespoon balsamic vinegar

Fresh basil, roughly chopped

1. Preheat oven to 400 degrees.

2. Line a baking sheet with foil.

3. Bring water to a boil in a wide saucepan.

4. Dip tomatoes into boiling water for 30-45 seconds to loosen skins. Transfer tomatoes to a bowl with ice water. Once cooled, peel tomatoes and cut in half lengthwise. Place cut side up on prepared pan and sprinkle with salt, garlic, and chopped herbs, followed by a drizzle of olive oil.

5. Roast in preheated oven for 20 minutes to allow herbs to be infused into tomatoes. Remove from oven; allow tomatoes to cool slightly.

6. Coarsely chop tomatoes and transfer along with any juices into a large stockpot. Add stock and bring to a boil. Reduce heat to a simmer and cook for 30 minutes.

7. Add balsamic vinegar and basil before serving.

8. If desired, soup may be lightly puréed.

9. Freezes well.

roasted-potato fennel soup

MEAT OR PARVE

When cooked with roasted potatoes, the fennel mellows and adds a fresh flavor to the soup.

4 pounds red potatoes, scrubbed and quartered

¼ cup plus 2 tablespoons good olive oil, divided

1 tablespoon minced garlic

1 tablespoon kosher salt

2 teaspoons fresh ground black pepper

4 cups chopped yellow onions (4 small onions)

4 cups chopped fennel bulb
(approximately 2 pounds)

3 quarts chicken or vegetable stock

1-2 cups soy milk, divided

Salt and pepper, to taste

1. Preheat oven to 400 degrees.

2. In a large bowl, toss potatoes with ¼ cup of the olive oil, garlic, salt, and pepper. Spread on a baking sheet and roast in preheated oven for 30-45 minutes, or until cooked through and soft.

3. Sauté onions and fennel in large stockpot with remaining 2 tablespoons olive oil for 10-15 minutes until wilted and starting to brown.

4. Add roasted potatoes (including any scrapings from the pan) and chicken or vegetable stock.

5. If desired, deglaze roasting pan with ¼ cup chicken or vegetable stock and transfer to stockpot. Cover and bring to a boil. Reduce heat and simmer uncovered for 1 hour.

6. Remove soup from heat and allow soup to cool slightly. Add 1 cup of soy milk.

7. Blend soup until smooth. Thin to desired consistency with additional soy milk.

8. Season to taste with salt and pepper.

butternut squash *and* leek soup

An unusual combination that makes an unforgettable soup.

3   medium butternut squash

4-5 tablespoons olive oil

    Salt

1   large onion, chopped

3   leeks, chopped

3   carrots, chopped

2   stalks celery, chopped

2   shallots, minced

4   cloves garlic, minced

6   teaspoons cider vinegar

5   quarts chicken or vegetable stock

4-6 teaspoons brown sugar

4   teaspoons curry powder or to taste

1   teaspoon cinnamon

2-3 fresh sage leaves

1. Preheat oven to 375 degrees.

2. Cut squash in half lengthwise and remove seeds. Drizzle with 1-2 tablespoons olive oil and salt; place face down on a cookie sheet. Roast squash in preheated oven for 30-45 minutes, or until squash is soft.

3. In a large stockpot, heat remaining olive oil and sauté onion, leeks, carrots, and celery for 5-7 minutes until soft. Add shallots and garlic; continue cooking for another minute. Increase heat and deglaze pan with vinegar. Add chicken or vegetable stock.

4. Scoop out squash from skin and add to pot, discarding the skin.

5. Add brown sugar, curry powder, cinnamon, and fresh sage leaves.

6. Cover pot and simmer approximately 45 minutes. Remove soup from heat and cool slightly.

7. Purée with an immersion blender or food processor.

8. Reheat to serve. Freezes well.

apple celery root soup

PARVE OR MEAT

Celery root is a fall root vegetable that has a delicious taste and gives this soup a creamy texture.

3-4 tablespoons olive oil

4 leeks, cut into ½-inch thick rounds (soak in several changes of cold water to remove sand; drain well before use)

6 celery roots, peeled and cut into large pieces

1 small potato, peeled and chopped

2 apples, peeled and chopped (any kind except Granny Smith)

4 cups vegetable or chicken stock

Salt and pepper, to taste

1. Heat oil in a stockpot; add leeks and sauté until soft.

2. Add celery root, potato, and apples. Cover pan and sweat vegetables 10 minutes until they begin to soften.

3. Add vegetable or chicken stock to cover vegetables. Replace cover and simmer until apples and vegetables are soft.

4. Purée with an immersion blender or food processor.

5. Season to taste with salt and pepper.

golden pepper purée

MEAT OR PARVE

This bright, yellow eye-catching soup makes for a beautiful presentation.

2	tablespoons olive oil
1	large onion, finely diced
2	cloves garlic, finely diced
2	teaspoons salt
1	teaspoon white pepper
1	stalk celery, finely diced
6	large yellow peppers, seeded and roughly chopped
2	potatoes, peeled and cubed
12	ounces chicken or vegetable broth
1	teaspoon paprika
2	scallions, finely chopped, for garnish
	Diced red pepper for garnish

1. Heat oil in a stockpot or Dutch oven.

2. Sauté onion, garlic, salt, and pepper for about 5 minutes until softened.

3. Stir in celery, yellow peppers, potatoes, and broth. Heat soup to a gentle boil. Lower heat and simmer, partially covered, about 20 minutes until vegetables are soft. Turn off heat and let cool.

4. Use blender or immersion blender to make a completely smooth purée. Simmer soup to blend favors. Thin with additional water or broth to desired consistency. Add paprika and season to taste with salt and pepper.

5. Garnish with chopped scallions or diced red pepper.

spicy red lentil soup

This hearty soup is ready in under an hour.

2   tablespoons olive oil

1   medium onion, finely chopped

2   cloves garlic, minced

1   teaspoon turmeric

1   teaspoon cumin

¼   teaspoon cayenne pepper

1   cup chopped tomatoes

4   cups water

1   cup dried red lentils

1   teaspoon salt

    Cilantro, chopped (optional)

1. Heat oil in a large stockpot. Sauté onion and garlic in oil until golden. Add spices and stir for 2-3 minutes.

2. Add tomatoes to the pot and continue cooking until they break down, stirring often to prevent sticking. Add water and lentils to the pot and let simmer for 45 minutes, stirring often. Season with salt.

3. Stir in cilantro just before serving, if desired.

hearty winter vegetable soup

PARVE OR MEAT

This soup celebrates the deep flavors of root vegetables and dark leafy greens.

2 tablespoons olive oil

4 leeks, halved lengthwise and cut into 1-inch slices

3 stalks celery, cut into ½-inch pieces

3 carrots, peeled and diced

2 cloves garlic, minced

½ teaspoon red pepper flakes

2 teaspoons kosher salt

5¼ cups chicken broth or vegetable stock

1½ cups water

2 potatoes, peeled and diced

1 small butternut squash, peeled and diced

1 bunch escarole, chopped (spinach, kale, or other greens may be substituted)

1 can (15 ounce) chickpeas, rinsed and drained

Juice of 1 lemon

2 tablespoons chopped fresh mint (optional)

2 tablespoons chopped fresh dill (optional)

Salt and pepper, to taste

1. Heat oil in a large stockpot or Dutch oven over medium-high heat. Add leeks, celery, carrots, garlic, red pepper flakes, and salt; sauté for about 5 minutes, or until leeks are softened.

2. Add chicken or vegetable stock and water. Bring to a boil.

3. Add potatoes and squash; return to a boil. Reduce heat and simmer partially covered for 15 minutes, or until vegetables are tender.

4. Stir in escarole (or other greens) and chickpeas. Return to a boil and cook about 3 minutes, until the greens are wilted.

5. Stir in lemon juice, along with mint, and dill (if using); simmer a few minutes to blend flavors.

6. Season soup, to taste, with salt and freshly ground pepper.

corn tortilla soup

MEAT

Mexico in a bowl! Delicious and fun!

3   tablespoons olive oil

1½   (7-inch) corn tortillas cut into 1-inch squares

1½   tablespoons minced fresh garlic

2   teaspoons minced white onion

1½   teaspoons minced jalapeño pepper

1   pound white or yellow corn kernels (2 cups)

1   can (6 ounce) tomato paste

2-2½   teaspoons cumin

2-3   teaspoons salt

⅛-½   teaspoon chili powder, to taste

1½   cups water

4   cups chicken stock

         Pinch curry powder

½   cup chopped fresh cilantro for garnish

1. Heat oil in a skillet over medium heat. Fry tortilla squares until they begin to crisp and turn golden yellow. Remove from skillet and drain.

2. Add garlic, onion, and jalapeño to the same skillet. Cook 1-2 minutes until onion becomes translucent.

3. Add ½ of the corn along with other ingredients (except garnish). Bring soup to a low even boil for 5 minutes.

4. Remove from heat. Use an immersion blender or food processor to purée until smooth. Return soup to burner and add remaining corn. Reheat soup gently until warmed through.

5. Garnish with corn tortilla chips and cilantro.

tomato cabbage soup

Like the sauce of a great stuffed cabbage without the meat. Warm and satisfying.

1 can (28 ounce) whole tomatoes, puréed, plus 1 can cold water

1 small cabbage, chopped in ½-inch pieces

1 large onion (or 1 bunch scallions), diced

1-2 tablespoons chopped fresh basil

4 cloves garlic, chopped

4 tablespoons olive oil

⅓ cup brown sugar

2-3 teaspoons kosher salt

2-3 teaspoons fresh ground black pepper

½-2 teaspoons chili powder, to taste

1. Heat oil in a large stockpot over medium heat. Sauté cabbage and onion until soft and wilted.

2. Add remaining ingredients and stir to combine. Bring soup to a gentle boil.

3. Loosely cover and reduce heat to simmer. Simmer for 20-30 minutes, stirring occasionally. If soup becomes too thick, thin with water.

4. Season to taste with additional salt, pepper, and chili powder.

gingered butternut squash apple soup

An Indian-inspired squash soup.

2   tablespoons olive oil

1   large onion, finely chopped

2   medium celery stalks, diced

2   Granny Smith apples, peeled, cored, and sliced

4   cups vegetable stock or water

1   whole butternut squash, peeled and sliced

1   teaspoon grated fresh ginger

1   teaspoon garam masala

½   teaspoon cinnamon

¼   teaspoon nutmeg

2   cups soy milk or whole milk

    Salt, to taste

1. Heat olive oil in large stockpot. Sauté onion and celery about 5 minutes.

2. Add remaining ingredients except soy milk or whole milk and salt. Bring soup to a boil, cover, and reduce heat to a simmer. Simmer soup for 40-45 minutes until vegetables are soft.

3. Stir in soy milk or milk and continue cooking until soup has thickened slightly.

4. Purée soup using an immersion blender or food processor.

5. Season to taste with salt.

6. Let soup stand a few hours or refrigerate overnight to allow the flavors to develop.

7. Serve warm or cold.

fusion wonton soup

The savory combination of ginger and beef-filled wontons is worth the extra effort.

6	cups chicken stock
1	2-inch piece of ginger, cleaned and julienned
4	scallions, sliced into 1-inch pieces
½	cup julienned carrots (optional)
½	cup julienned pea pods (optional)
1	tablespoon sesame oil

wontons:

½	pound ground beef
1	tablespoon minced ginger
2	tablespoons minced onion or scallion
1	tablespoon minced garlic
2	tablespoons tamari or soy sauce
2	tablespoons chopped cilantro (parsley may be substituted)
2	teaspoons sugar
1	tablespoon sesame oil
1	teaspoon cornstarch or arrowroot
¼	cup shredded carrot (optional)
2	teaspoons sherry
¼-½	teaspoon hot sauce (optional)
½	teaspoon pepper
20	small round or square wonton wrappers (rice paper wrappers may be substituted—soak each briefly in water to soften before use)
1	tablespoon cornstarch mixed with 3 tablespoons water
	Cornstarch for dusting wontons

1. To prepare soup, place chicken stock, ginger, and scallions in a wide pot with a lid. Bring stock to a gentle simmer and cover.

2. Continue cooking for 20 minutes.

3. Prepare wontons while the soup is cooking. Gently mix all ingredients except wonton wrappers until well combined. Mixture will be slightly sticky.

4. To assemble wontons, sprinkle a cookie sheet with cornstarch.

5. Lay several wonton skins on a separate work surface. Brush half of each wonton with a little of the cornstarch and water slurry. Place a teaspoon of filling in the center of the wonton. Fold dough over filling and press edges to seal. (Wontons may be frozen uncooked.) If using rice paper, do not brush with cornstarch. Fold softened wrappers around filling, pressing edges to seal.

6. Place completed wontons on prepared cookie sheet. Do not stack wontons without sprinkling with additional cornstarch.

7. To cook, add wontons (frozen or freshly prepared) to simmering soup and cover pot. Cook for 10-15 minutes until wontons are cooked through. Add carrots and pea pods (if using) to soup along with wontons. If using rice paper, steam wontons separately before adding to soup.

8. Add sesame oil to soup just before serving.

9. Alternately, wontons may be steamed separately in a lightly oiled steamer and rewarmed briefly in the soup before serving.

salads

moroccan carrot salad

Now you can make this classic Middle Eastern dish at home.

2 pounds carrots, sliced

½ cup chopped parsley

3-4 cloves garlic, crushed

Juice of 2 lemons

¼ cup oil

¾ teaspoon cumin

1 teaspoon paprika

½ teaspoon cayenne pepper

Salt, to taste

1. Cook carrots until barely tender.

2. Place all ingredients except carrots in a closed container and shake vigorously to combine.

3. Toss carrots with dressing. Marinate for a few hours or overnight.

4. Serve chilled.

orange, basil, and olive salad

A salad with oranges and olives? This unique combination packs a lot of flavor and the ingredients complement each other beautifully.

5	large seedless oranges
1	small shallot, finely chopped
⅛	teaspoon cayenne pepper
1	teaspoon smoked paprika
½	teaspoon chopped garlic
3	tablespoons olive oil
1	tablespoon red wine or sherry vinegar
1	teaspoon salt
	Freshly ground black pepper
12-14	fresh basil leaves, chopped
⅓	cup chopped parsley
12	pitted black kalamata olives

1. Peel oranges, paring away all exterior white pulp. Slice each orange crosswise into circles, approximately ½-inch thick. Set aside along with any accumulated juices.

2. In a salad bowl, whisk together shallots, cayenne, smoked paprika, garlic, olive oil, vinegar, salt, and pepper.

3. Add oranges, accumulated juice, basil, parsley, and olives to bowl with dressing and toss gently to blend.

4. Serve cold or at room temperature.

panzanella salad

The bread soaks up the flavor of the vegetables and dressing, and delivers a filling and colorful salad.

1	cup diced plum tomatoes
½	cup diced yellow tomato
½	cup diced red onion
¼	cup pitted black olives
2	tablespoons capers
¼	cup chopped parsley
2	tablespoons chopped fresh basil
⅓	cup olive oil
3	tablespoons sliced garlic
⅛-½	teaspoon hot red pepper flakes
2	tablespoons lemon juice
1	tablespoon balsamic vinegar
½	teaspoon dried oregano
2	cups crusty stale bread, diced
	Salt and pepper, to taste

1. In a large bowl, combine plum tomatoes, yellow tomatoes, red onion, olives, capers, parsley, and basil. Set aside.

2. Heat oil in a small saucepan. Sauté garlic and red pepper flakes until garlic turns golden.

3. Remove pan from fire and stir in lemon juice, vinegar, and oregano.

4. Pour dressing over vegetables and toss.

5. Two hours before serving, toss cubed bread into salad. Season to taste with salt and pepper.

6. Serve room temperature.

arugula *and* cheese salad *with* lemon shallot dressing

DAIRY

An elegant dairy appetizer.

salad:

2-3 tablespoons canola oil

2 ounces baby arugula

2½ ounces mixed greens

3 Persian cucumbers, sliced in half moons

1 log goat, halloumi, or kashkaval cheese, sliced into 1-inch pieces

1 egg, beaten

 Flavored breadcrumbs

dressing:

¼ cup fresh lemon juice

1 small shallot, minced

½ teaspoon kosher salt

¼ teaspoon pepper, to taste

2 teaspoons honey

¼ cup olive oil

1. Heat canola oil in frying pan or skillet.

2. Dip cheese in egg, then breadcrumbs. Fry breaded cheese until golden.

3. Combine all dressing ingredients and whisk thoroughly. Pour dressing over greens and cucumbers, tossing to coat.

4. To serve, plate greens with sliced cheese on top.

fennel *and* bulgur salad

PARVE

A fresh summer salad perfect as a Shabbat side dish.

1   cup medium-fine bulgur or cracked wheat

1   cup fresh lemon juice, plus more to taste

½   cup extra-virgin olive oil

4   cloves garlic, minced

2   teaspoons salt, divided

8   scallions (white and green parts), thinly sliced

1   cup chopped flat-leaf parsley

½   cup chopped fresh dill

⅓   cup chopped fresh mint

2   English cucumbers, peeled, seeded, and diced
     ½-inch thick

¼   teaspoon freshly ground black pepper

1   large fennel bulb

⅓   cup pine nuts, toasted

    Salt and pepper, to taste

    Juice of 1 lemon

1. Place bulgur or cracked wheat in large salad bowl.

2. Whisk lemon juice, oil, garlic, and 1 teaspoon of salt. Drizzle over bulgur.

3. Add scallions, parsley, dill, mint, and cucumber.

4. Sprinkle remaining teaspoon of salt and ¼ teaspoon pepper over top.

5. Cover bulgur with plastic wrap. Refrigerate for 24-48 hours.

6. Cut fennel bulb in half lengthwise, then cut halves crosswise into paper-thin slices. Add fennel and pine nuts to salad.

7. Season to taste with salt, pepper, and lemon juice.

8. Best served at room temperature.

mango, jicama, *and* cucumber salad

Jicama is crunchy, slightly sweet, and full of fresh flavor, adding a special touch to this springtime salad.

2   ripe mangoes, peeled and cubed

1   medium jicama, peeled and cubed

1   medium English cucumber, cubed

¼   cup lime juice

Zest of 1 lime

2   tablespoons honey

1   cup canola oil

Salt, to taste

Sprig fresh dill for garnish

1. Combine mangoes, jicama, and cucumber in a bowl.

2. Mix lime juice, zest, and honey in a blender or food processor. With the blender or processor running, slowly drizzle in canola oil, until slightly thickened.

3. Season to taste with salt.

4. Pour dressing over mango mixture, tossing to coat. Garnish with dill.

mustard-crusted beef tenderloin *and* arugula salad MEAT

A perfect summer main-course salad or a year-round appetizer.

beef:

¼ cup coarse-grain mustard

¾ teaspoon dry mustard

2¼ teaspoons packed dark brown sugar

¾ teaspoon coarsely ground black pepper

½ teaspoon grated lemon zest

1 pound London broil or chuck roast
   Salt and pepper, to taste

1 tablespoon oil

salad:

½ pound wax or green beans, cut into 2-inch pieces

4 cups baby arugula

1 small red onion, thinly sliced

dressing:

1½ tablespoons balsamic vinegar

1 tablespoon fresh lemon juice

¼ teaspoon Dijon mustard
   Salt and pepper, to taste

¼ cup olive oil

1. Preheat oven to 425 degrees.

2. Combine mustards, brown sugar, pepper, and lemon zest. Set aside.

3. Pat beef dry and season with salt and pepper.

4. Heat oil in heavy skillet over medium-high heat until very hot. Sear beef on both sides until browned.

5. Transfer meat to greased shallow baking pan and coat with mustard mixture. Roast until medium rare, about 20 minutes.

6. Transfer to cutting board and let stand until cool.

7. Boil beans in salted water about 5 minutes until tender. Drain beans and place in an ice bath to stop cooking process. Drain.

8. In large bowl, combine beans with arugula and onion slices.

9. Prepare dressing by whisking together vinegar, lemon juice, and mustard.

10. Season to taste with salt and pepper.

11. In a slow stream, add oil, whisking, until emulsified.

12. Remove 2 tablespoons dressing and set aside. Pour remaining dressing over salad and toss to coat. Transfer to a serving platter.

13. Thinly slice beef and layer on salad. Drizzle with reserved dressing.

pesto potato salad

A new spin on an old classic.

potatoes:

3   pounds small red or fingerling potatoes

2   scallions, thinly sliced

4   small dill pickles or cornichons, chopped

pesto:

½   cup fresh basil leaves

⅓   cup extra-virgin olive oil

2   tablespoons pine nuts, toasted

3   tablespoons white wine vinegar

Juice of 1 lemon

2   tablespoons water

1   teaspoon salt

½   teaspoon ground black pepper

2   cloves garlic

1. Boil potatoes in lightly salted water about 15 minutes until fork tender. Drain and let cool. (Potatoes can be made earlier and refrigerated; bring to room temperature before assembling.)

2. Combine pesto ingredients in food processor until emulsified into a thick, creamy dressing.

3. Slice potatoes in half. Pour dressing over potatoes, scallions, and pickles, tossing to coat.

4. Let marinate 30 minutes.

edamame rimon salad

PARVE

A modern combination of edamame and pomegranate seeds.

salad:

16 ounces frozen shelled edamame, thawed

1½-2 cups fresh or frozen corn, cooked

1 can hearts of palm, drained and sliced

Seeds from 2 pomegranates, about 2 cups

1 (10 ounce) package frozen artichokes, thawed, or 1 cup green beans, cooked (optional)

dressing:

3 tablespoons olive oil

3 tablespoons lemon juice

1 tablespoon honey

½ teaspoon salt

¼ teaspoon pepper

¼ teaspoon dried basil or 1 teaspoon chopped fresh basil

1. Mix salad ingredients in a bowl.

2. Combine dressing ingredients and mix well; pour over salad.

3. Salad can be assembled several hours to 1 day ahead.

spinach *and* apple salad

Easy, gorgeous, and delicious.

salad:

1   bag (10 ounce) fresh spinach

2   crisp unpeeled red skinned apples, cut into matchstick slices

Slivered almonds

dressing:

¼   cup chopped onion

3   tablespoons cider vinegar

3   tablespoons white wine vinegar

1   tablespoon sesame seeds

¼   teaspoon paprika

2   tablespoons honey

⅓   cup olive oil

Salt and pepper, to taste

1. Place spinach, apples, and almonds in a bowl.

2. Combine all dressing ingredients.

3. Pour over salad and toss.

avocado *and* pink grapefruit salad

PARVE

Exquisite and refreshing.

salad:

Leaves from 1 head arugula

2   ripe avocados, halved, pitted, peeled, thinly sliced

2   medium Ruby Red grapefruits, all peel and white pith cut away, segments cut from between membranes

dressing:

2   tablespoons white grape juice

2½ teaspoons apple cider vinegar

2   tablespoons fresh lime juice

1   shallot, minced

¼   cup avocado or grape seed oil

¼   cup olive oil

Salt and pepper, to taste

1. Arrange lettuce on platter; top with avocado and grapefruit.

2. Whisk first 4 ingredients of dressing in small bowl to blend. Gradually whisk in both oils.

3. Season dressing to taste with salt and pepper. Drizzle dressing over salad.

thai mango slaw *with* pecans

An exotic alternative to traditional coleslaw. Use a firm mango to achieve the best results.

1   large firm mango, peeled, pitted and sliced
        into thin spears

1-1¼ pounds savoy or red cabbage, thinly sliced

1   red pepper, julienned

½   red onion, thinly sliced

6   tablespoons fresh lime juice

¼   cup rice vinegar

2   tablespoons oil

½   teaspoon salt

¼   cup fresh mint leaves, thinly sliced

¼   cup coarsely chopped toasted pecans

1. Toss mango, cabbage, red pepper, and onion in a large bowl.

2. Whisk lime juice, vinegar, oil, salt, and pepper in a smaller bowl and pour over slaw. Marinate in the refrigerator for 1-2 hours.

3. Toss with mint leaves and sprinkle with pecans before serving.

warm mushroom salad *with* cherries

The mixture of temperatures, textures, and flavors makes this dish unique.

2 tablespoons finely diced shallots

3 tablespoons sherry or white wine vinegar

½ teaspoon salt

7 tablespoons extra-virgin olive oil, divided

2 pounds mushrooms (cremini or a mix of wild mushrooms), cleaned and sliced

1 teaspoon fresh thyme or ¼ teaspoon dried thyme, halved

6 ounces salad greens such as frisée, arugula, or a mix of your choice

½ cup mix of fresh herbs such as chives, tarragon, basil, or dill (optional)

12-14 fresh cherries, pitted and halved (can substitute dried cherries)

Salt and pepper, to taste

1. Whisk shallots, vinegar, and ½ teaspoon salt together. Set aside for 5 minutes to soften shallots.

2. Whisk in 5 tablespoons of the olive oil.

3. Heat remaining 2-3 tablespoons olive oil in large sauté pan over medium-high heat. Add mushrooms and half of the thyme. Season with salt and pepper. Sauté for 5 minutes until mushrooms are softened but not limp.

4. Spread salad greens on a plate and sprinkle fresh herbs on top, if using.

5. Spoon hot mushrooms over salad greens and add cherries.

6. Pour dressing over salad and toss carefully.

7. Season to taste with salt, pepper, oil, and vinegar.

pear *and* pomegranate salad

The red onion in this salad brings balance to the sweetness and tartness of the pears, cranberry juice, and pomegranate.

3	Anjou or Bartlett pears
1	cup cranberry juice
8-10	ounces baby arugula or baby lettuce
½	small red onion, thinly sliced
½	cup chopped honey-glazed pecans
2	handfuls pomegranate seeds
¼	cup pomegranate syrup
⅛	cup red wine or balsamic vinegar
⅔	cup olive oil
1	teaspoon stone ground mustard

1. Cut pears in half, then cut each half into three wedges. Cut out seeds and cut each wedge into thirds crosswise.

2. Place in a bowl with cranberry juice and let marinate for 30 minutes to 1 hour.

3. Pour pomegranate syrup, vinegar, oil, and mustard into a jar with a tight-fitting lid; shake well.

4. Combine arugula, red onion, pecans, and pomegranate seeds in a bowl.

5. Add pears, dress with vinaigrette, and toss.

marinated kale salad

Kale is a dark leafy green that is loaded with vitamins. Marinating in lemon juice and oil softens the kale and brings out its fresh flavor.

2   large bunches kale

5   tablespoons olive oil

    Juice of 1 lemon

    Zest of 1 lemon (optional)

1   teaspoon salt

1   teaspoon pepper

1   ripe mango, peeled and cubed (optional)

½   cup pomegranate seeds (optional)

1. Trim and discard stalks from kale. Wash trimmed kale leaves very well in several changes of water. Drain well and chop into bite-size pieces.

2. Place kale in a large zip-top bag with olive oil, lemon juice, and zest, if using. Season with salt and pepper.

3. Massage kale in bag until softened. Refrigerate, and let marinate for 2 to 3 hours or overnight.

4. Transfer kale to a bowl and serve sprinkled with mango or pomegranate seeds.

a trio of dressings

Everyone could use a few dips or dressings in their repertoire to perk up a green salad or steamed veggies.

honey mustard dressing:

¼   cup honey

¼   cup Dijon mustard

1   clove garlic, minced

4   tablespoons oil

3   tablespoons balsamic vinegar

1   tablespoon chopped dill (optional)

    Salt and pepper, to taste

1. Mix ingredients in a bowl or jar until smooth and emulsified. Store refrigerated for up to 3 weeks.

tangy japanese restaurant dressing:

½   carrot, cleaned and coarsely chopped

¼   cup rice wine vinegar

4   tablespoons oil

1   tablespoon sesame oil

1   teaspoon honey or sugar

1   clove garlic

3   scallions, white parts only

1   tablespoon chopped ginger

2   teaspoons Tamari or soy sauce

    Salt and pepper, to taste

1. Combine all ingredients and purée in a food processor or with an immersion blender. Store refrigerated for up to 1 week.

creamy pesto dressing *and* dip:

2-3 cloves garlic

½   cup basil leaves, cleaned and dried

2   tablespoons pine nuts or raw cashews (shelled pumpkin or sunflower seeds may be substituted)

⅓   cup olive oil

    Juice of 1 lemon

2   tablespoons mayonnaise

¼   cup rice wine vinegar

    Pinch sugar

    Salt and pepper, to taste

1. Combine ingredients and purée in a food processor or with an immersion blender until smooth. Thin with a few tablespoons water if sauce is too thick. Store refrigerated for up to 1 week.

vegetables

fasulia *(green beans with tomatoes and garlic)*

A simple and colorful Sephardic dish that is an ideal side or the star of a vegetarian meal served over rice or quinoa.

2 tablespoons olive oil

1 large or 2 medium onions, finely chopped

8-10 cloves garlic (adjust to taste), chopped into eighths

2 pounds fresh green beans, trimmed

2 large tomatoes, finely chopped

1 teaspoon salt

1 teaspoon pepper

1 teaspoon paprika

1. Preheat olive oil in a large pot. Add onions and sauté until soft.

2. Add garlic; let cook for about 1 minute, being careful not to burn.

3. Add string beans, tomatoes, salt, pepper, paprika, and enough water to just cover vegetables. Bring to a simmer.

4. Reduce heat and simmer covered for about 10 minutes. Beans should be tender, but not overdone; they will continue to cook after heat is off. Adjust seasoning.

flash-fried brussels sprouts *with* smoky vinaigrette

"Mini-cabbages" expand into crispy, nutty, and slightly sweet "chips" when flash-fried and seasoned.

Canola oil for deep-frying

smoky vinaigrette:

1   clove garlic, minced

¼   cup red wine vinegar

1   tablespoon honey

1   teaspoon smoked paprika

1   teaspoon Dijon mustard

2   scallions, white and green parts, thinly sliced on the bias

½   cup coarsely chopped walnut pieces, toasted

½   cup extra-virgin olive oil

brussels sprouts:

1   pound Brussels sprouts, trimmed and quartered lengthwise

2   cups loosely packed flat-leaf parsley leaves

Salt, to taste

Freshly ground black pepper, to taste

1. Pour enough oil into a medium pot so that the oil comes 3 inches up the sides.

2. Heat oil to 350 degrees.

3. While oil is heating, whisk together garlic, red wine vinegar, honey, paprika, mustard, scallions, walnuts, and extra-virgin olive oil in a bowl large enough to toss all of the Brussels sprouts. Keep the bowl near the stovetop.

4. Working in batches, deep-fry Brussels sprouts about 3 minutes until the edges begin to curl and brown. Give the contents of the pot a stir. When the color of the Brussels sprouts become a deeper, more saturated shade of green (about 30 seconds to 1 minute), remove them with a slotted spoon and place directly in the bowl of dressing. Repeat with remaining Brussels sprouts.

5. Add parsley and toss to coat.

6. Season to taste with salt and pepper.

wild mushroom *and* potato mash

A chic update on a classic.

8   dried shiitake or other dried mushrooms

¼   pound mixed fresh mushrooms, sliced

4   tablespoons olive oil, divided

⅓   cup chopped onion

1   small clove garlic, minced

1¼ pounds russet potatoes, peeled and cut into 1-inch cubes

¾   cup dry white wine

½   teaspoon kosher salt

1   teaspoon chopped fresh dill

1   teaspoon chopped fresh thyme

2   tablespoons chopped fresh parsley

Pepper, to taste

1. Soak dried mushrooms in enough warm water to cover for approximately 30 minutes. Remove mushrooms, rinse to remove grit, and slice. Reserve soaking liquid.

2. Heat 2 tablespoons of the oil in a large pot and sauté chopped onion until softened.

3. Add garlic and potatoes. Pour in white wine. Add salt and cover the pot.

4. Simmer on medium-low heat for 10 minutes. Add soaked mushrooms and reserved liquid. Stir and cover again. Continue simmering, stirring occasionally, for another 10 minutes. Potatoes should be completely tender.

5. Heat remaining oil in a skillet. Add dill, thyme, parsley, and sliced mushrooms; sauté, stirring constantly, until mushrooms are tender. Set aside.

6. When potatoes are cooked, add sautéed mushrooms to the pot and simmer uncovered for a few more minutes, stirring often until potatoes are lightly mashed.

7. Add pepper to taste, and more salt if needed.

spaghetti squash *with* tomatoes *and* baby spinach

As delicious as it is beautiful. Add your favorite meatballs or chickpeas for a protein-packed, fully balanced main dish.

1   spaghetti squash

2   tablespoons extra-virgin olive oil

1   pint fresh cherry tomatoes or
     1 can (28 ounce) chopped tomatoes, drained

1   medium onion, finely chopped

2   cloves garlic, finely minced

2   teaspoons salt

½   teaspoon freshly ground black pepper

1   teaspoon cumin

½   teaspoon smoked paprika

1   can (8 ounce) tomato sauce

2   cups baby spinach leaves

    Shredded Parmesan (optional)

1. Preheat oven to 375 degrees. Slice squash lengthwise. Place squash, cut sides down, onto a cookie sheet. Roast 45-60 minutes or until squash is soft. Remove squash from oven. Let cool for 10 minutes. Remove seeds with a spoon. Using a fork, scrape out the flesh from the shell and place in a bowl.

2. Add oil to a stockpot or Dutch oven; add tomatoes, onion, garlic, salt, pepper, cumin, and paprika. Cook for 5-7 minutes.

3. Add squash and sauté for an additional 5 minutes.

4. Add tomato sauce and spinach. Mix thoroughly; season to taste with salt, pepper, and spices.

5. Partially cover pot and simmer for an additional 5 minutes or until all ingredients are incorporated.

6. Sprinkle with Parmesan, if serving as dairy dish.

Note: *Spinach not included in photograph.*

beer-battered green beans *with* garlic aïoli

A terrific alternative to French fries or a great appetizer.

green beans:

⅔   cup beer

½   cup flour

2   tablespoons cornstarch

½   teaspoon salt

1   pound green beans, trimmed

2   cups canola oil

garlic aïoli:

¼   cup mayonnaise

½   teaspoon Dijon mustard

1   clove garlic, crushed

2   tablespoons chopped fresh flat-leaf parsley

Salt and pepper, to taste

1. In a large bowl, whisk together beer, flour, cornstarch, and salt. Let rest for 10 minutes.

2. Submerge beans in ice water for 2-3 minutes to maintain color. Pat beans dry (this makes them extra-crisp).

3. In a large pot, heat oil to 375 degrees, or when a drop of batter sizzles immediately and rises to the surface.

4. Whisk batter again, add green beans, and toss to coat.

5. Working in 4 batches and using tongs, gently lower beans into oil. Fry, turning halfway through, about 3 minutes, until golden brown. Let drain on paper towels.

6. Season to taste with salt.

7. To prepare garlic aïoli, whisk together mayonnaise, mustard, parsley, and garlic in a small bowl. Season to taste with salt and pepper.

8. Serve green beans with garlic aïoli.

citrus roasted carrots

The orange and cumin highlight the flavor of an everyday staple.

1½ pounds baby carrots

3   tablespoons extra-virgin olive oil, divided

½   teaspoon kosher salt

¼   teaspoon pepper

2   oranges

¼   teaspoon ground cumin

2   scallions (white and light green parts), chopped

¼   cup toasted pine nuts

1. Preheat oven to 400 degrees.

2. Combine carrots, 2 tablespoons of oil, salt, and pepper in a bowl. Spread into a single layer on a rimmed baking sheet. Roast in preheated oven about 30 minutes until carrots are tender.

3. Meanwhile, separate oranges by cutting away peel and white pith. Cut on both sides of each segment, freeing the segments from the membrane. Place the segments in a bowl, then squeeze the membranes over oranges to extract any remaining juice. Stir in cumin, scallions, and remaining oil.

4. Arrange carrots on a platter and spoon orange mixture over the top. Sprinkle with toasted pine nuts. Serve hot or at room temperature.

asparagus *with* lemon pesto

An easy, elegant way to enjoy asparagus.

asparagus:

1   bunch asparagus, ends removed

lemon pesto:

2   cloves garlic, chopped

Juice of 1 lemon

1-1½ teaspoons honey

Salt and pepper, to taste

½   cup finely chopped walnuts

½   cup olive oil

1. Place asparagus in shallow pan with salted boiling water. Boil 2-3 minutes until color has just turned bright green and asparagus are crisp but tender. Immediately remove asparagus from boiling water and place into ice water to stop the cooking. Once cooled, dry off asparagus and set aside.

2. To make pesto, mix together garlic, lemon juice, honey, salt, pepper, and ¼ cup of the walnuts in a food processor or blender. Slowly add olive oil in a stream. Taste and adjust seasoning as needed. Pesto should be the consistency of a thick dressing, but still pourable.

3. To serve, place asparagus on a platter, pour dressing over asparagus, and sprinkle remaining crushed walnuts on top.

balsamic *and* basil beets

This stunning root vegetable is packed with antioxidants. Roasting the beets brings out their sweetness.

2 pounds beets, unpeeled

1 tablespoon olive oil

2 tablespoons chopped fresh basil

2 tablespoons balsamic vinegar

1 tablespoon brown sugar

¼ teaspoon salt

1. Preheat oven to 450 degrees.

2. Toss beets with olive oil and place in a 9x13-inch roasting pan.

3. Roast for 1-1½ hours, until easily pierced with a fork.

4. Cool beets, peel, and dice.

5. Mix basil, vinegar, sugar, and salt in a bowl.

6. Toss beets with mixture. Serve at room temperature.

butternut squash *with* mushrooms *and* shallots

Given its similarity to yams, butternut squash usually shows up in sweeter side dishes. This dish offers a savory alternative.

2 large butternut squash, peeled, seeded, and cut into 2-inch cubes

10 shallots, peeled, sliced into ¼-inch rounds

3 tablespoons extra-virgin olive oil, divided

17 cremini mushrooms, sliced into ¼-inch pieces

10 shiitake mushrooms, sliced into ¼-inch pieces

Kosher salt and pepper, to taste

1. Steam squash until soft, not mushy.

2. Sauté shallots in 2 tablespoons olive oil until caramelized.

3. Add mushrooms to shallots and sauté with remaining 1 tablespoon oil. Season to taste with kosher salt and pepper.

4. Mix squash with shallots and mushrooms; adjust salt and pepper.

5. Can be made a day in advance; cover well and refrigerate. Rewarm, covered, in a 350 degree oven for 20 minutes.

cauliflower mash

A creamy, no-guilt side dish.

1   large Yukon gold potato, peeled and cut into
    ¾-inch chunks

1   head cauliflower (about 2¼ pounds), trimmed
    and cut into florets

2   cups water

2   teaspoons olive oil

1   clove garlic, crushed

¼   cup loosely packed fresh parsley leaves,
    chopped

¾   teaspoon salt

¼   teaspoon black pepper

¼   teaspoon cumin

¼   teaspoon chili powder (optional)

1. Place potato and cauliflower in a 4-quart saucepan. Add water; cover and heat to boiling over high heat.

2. Reduce heat to low; cover and simmer about 20 minutes or until potato and cauliflower are fork-tender, stirring once halfway through cooking.

3. Drain vegetables, reserving ¼ cup cooking liquid.

4. In same saucepan, heat oil and sauté garlic over medium-low heat, stirring until garlic is golden. Reduce heat to low; return vegetables to saucepan to gently rewarm.

5. Coarsely mash vegetables, adding some reserved cooking liquid if mixture seems dry. If you prefer a smooth texture, use an immersion blender until the mixture is smooth.

6. Stir in parsley, salt, pepper, cumin, and chili powder, if using.

middle eastern leeks

This dish puts the leek in the spotlight and shows off its delicious versatility.

2 tablespoons olive oil

1 large onion, chopped

8 leeks, dark green tops trimmed off, washed and quartered lengthwise

3 cloves garlic, minced

1 can (28 ounce) crushed tomatoes

1 cup chicken or vegetable stock

½ teaspoon salt

½ tablespoon sugar

Juice of 1 lemon

2 medium potatoes, peeled and cubed

1. Heat oil in a saucepan over medium heat. Add onion and sauté 5 minutes.

2. Add leeks and continue sautéing another 3-4 minutes.

3. Reduce heat and add garlic, stirring well and cooking an additional 3 minutes.

4. Add tomatoes, stock, salt, sugar, and lemon juice to onion leek mixture. Increase heat and bring the mixture to a boil.

5. Reduce the heat to low; cover and simmer 15 minutes.

6. Add potato cubes to the saucepan. Continue cooking, covered, for 20-25 minutes, stirring occasionally to ensure that leeks do not burn. Check to make sure potatoes are just cooked through.

7. Remove lid, increase heat, and simmer briskly 5-10 minutes until most of the liquid has evaporated.

crispy kale chips

Nutty, crispy, and loaded with vitamins, a perfect family snack.

1   pound kale, tough stems removed, torn into bite-size pieces

1-2 tablespoons olive oil

  Salt, to taste

1. Preheat oven to 350 degrees.

2. Line a baking sheet with parchment paper.

3. Place kale leaves into a salad spinner and spin all of the water out. Pour out the water and repeat until kale is completely dry. Place kale in a single layer on prepared baking sheet.

4. Drizzle olive oil over kale leaves and toss to coat the leaves evenly.

5. Bake for 12-20 minutes until leaves are crisp. Test after 12 minutes to check whether the kale is paper-thin and crackly. If the leaves are still a bit soft, continue baking for 3-5 minutes. Be careful not to let the leaves become dark brown or the kale will be bitter.

6. Remove from oven, sprinkle with salt, and serve.

marinated broccoli

An easy, no-cook way to serve this super-food.

1   clove garlic, crushed

½   teaspoon salt

¼   cup vegetable or canola oil

1   tablespoon Dijon mustard

⅛   teaspoon pepper

¼   cup apple cider vinegar

3   tablespoons brown sugar

1   head broccoli, cut into florets

1. Combine all ingredients except broccoli and transfer to a large zip-top bag.

2. Place broccoli in a large zip-top bag with mixture. Marinate in the refrigerator for 2 hours or overnight.

smoky braised portobello mushrooms

The marinade makes this dish truly special.

smoky marinade:

¼ cup low-sodium tamari or soy sauce

1 teaspoon toasted sesame oil

2 tablespoons apple juice

1 teaspoon maple syrup

¼ teaspoon liquid smoke

1 teaspoon crushed garlic

¼ cup water

Dash salt

Pepper, to taste

braised mushrooms:

3-4 (5-inch cap) portobello mushrooms, stemmed

Smoky marinade

1 tablespoon olive oil

¼ cup water

1. Mix all marinade ingredients.

2. Cut mushrooms in half and soak them in marinade for at least 1 hour. Drain mushrooms and reserve marinade.

3. Heat oil in a skillet. Place mushrooms in oil top side down and brown them over medium-high heat.

4. Add water and ¼ cup of the reserved marinade.

5. Turn mushrooms over and reduce heat to low. Cover and cook for 15 minutes. Check periodically to see if liquid has evaporated, adding the rest of marinade as needed.

roasted vegetable tart

A terrific make-ahead option that is best served at room temperature. Start this dish at least 3 hours or a day before you plan to serve.

2   tomatoes, (Roma or beefsteak), cut into
      1-inch slices

½   cup olive oil, for brushing vegetables

      Salt

2   cloves garlic, chopped

1   large eggplant, cut into ½-inch slices

2   zucchinis, cut into ½-inch slices

2   yellow squash, cut into ½-inch slices

2   red or yellow peppers, cored and quartered
      lengthwise (optional)

1   cup basil (about 20 basil leaves), cleaned

      Pepper

1. Preheat oven to 400 degrees.

2. Brush 2 or 3 large baking sheets with olive oil.

3. Place tomato slices on a baking sheet. Brush with oil and sprinkle lightly with salt. Sprinkle tomatoes with chopped garlic.

4. Place eggplant slices in one layer on another baking sheet, brush with oil, and sprinkle with salt.

5. Roast 15 minutes until eggplant is browned and tomatoes have softened. Transfer vegetables to a plate to cool.

6. Repeat with remaining vegetables, omitting garlic, and roasting each vegetable on a separate baking sheet, about 15 minutes until softened and beginning to brown.

7. To assemble tart, oil a large tart pan or deep pie pan. Cover the bottom of the prepared dish with about ½ of the eggplant slices. Season eggplant with pepper. Layer zucchini, yellow squash, tomato, red or yellow pepper (if using), and basil on top of the eggplant base. Season each layer with additional salt and pepper.

8. For the top layer, cover vegetables with the remaining eggplant.

9. Place a plate on top of vegetables. Place a heavy weight such as a can of tomatoes on top of the plate.

10. Let tart stand weighted for about 3 hours at room temperature or refrigerated up to 2 days ahead.

11. To serve, bring to room temperature.

breads, grains, *and* pasta

breads, grains, *and* pasta

amazing beer bread

This no-fuss recipe is perfect for when you don't have much prep time.

3   cups flour

1   tablespoon baking powder

3   tablespoons sugar

1   teaspoon salt

12 ounces beer at room temperature

¼   cup unsalted butter, melted (optional)

1. Preheat oven to 375 degrees.

2. In a mixing bowl, combine dry ingredients. Add beer all at once, mixing as little as possible. Batter should be lumpy.

3. Pour into an oiled 9x5x3-inch loaf pan. If desired, brush with melted butter.

4. Bake in preheated oven 35-40 minutes. Best eaten warm, the same day.

biscuits

DAIRY OR PARVE

These biscuits are scrumptious. This recipe doubles easily, which you may want to consider, once they have all disappeared in minutes.

2 cups unbleached white flour
(or mixture white and whole wheat)

2 teaspoons baking powder

1 teaspoon salt

1-2 tablespoons sugar (optional)

5 tablespoons cold butter or margarine, cut into small pieces

½-¾ cup or more milk, rice milk, almond milk, or water

1. Preheat oven to 400 degrees. (If using margarine, preheat to 375 degrees.)

2. Place flour, baking powder, salt, and sugar in the bowl of a food processor. Add butter or margarine. Pulse quickly several times until butter is incorporated and mixture is crumbly.

3. Transfer to a bowl. Add milk and mix to moisten. Add more liquid if mixture is dry. Lightly gather dough into a rough ball.

4. Transfer to a floured board. Gently knead dough by patting dough into a flattened disc. Fold dough into thirds like a letter. Pat or roll dough into a ½-inch-thick rectangle, flouring lightly to prevent sticking. Cut biscuits into 2-inch rounds using a biscuit cutter or a small glass dipped in flour.

5. Transfer cut biscuits to a parchment-lined cookie sheet. Gather scraps and roll dough out again and repeat step 4, handling as little as possible.

6. Bake in preheated oven for 10-15 minutes until golden and puffy.

whole wheat olive rosemary loaf

A delicious Italian-inspired bread. Perfect with pasta and wine.

2   cups whole-wheat flour

1   cup unbleached bread flour

2   teaspoons salt

½   teaspoon yeast

2   cups cold water

2   cups pitted black olives

3-4 tablespoons rosemary leaves from 3 stems

1. In a large mixing bowl, combine flours, salt, yeast, and water; mix well. Cover bowl with plastic wrap and then with a clean towel. Place in a cool, dry place to rise for 18 hours.

2. When dough has almost tripled in size, stir in olives and rosemary leaves. Dough will be stringy.

3. Preheat oven to 475 degrees.

4. Spray a loaf pan or pot with olive oil spray.

5. Transfer dough to prepared pan. Cover with foil and bake in preheated oven for 30 minutes, then uncover and bake for an additional 30 minutes until bread is golden brown.

pumpkin cranberry bread

Another yeast-free bread recipe that is rich on flavor but not time-consuming. A great after-school snack.

2   large eggs, slightly beaten

2   cups sugar

½   cup oil

1   cup solid pack pumpkin

2¼ cups flour

1½ teaspoons ginger

1½ teaspoons cinnamon

¼   teaspoon nutmeg

¼   teaspoon cloves

1   teaspoon baking soda

½   teaspoon salt

1   cup chopped cranberries

½   cup chopped walnuts (optional)

1. Preheat oven to 350 degrees.

2. Combine eggs, sugar, oil, and pumpkin; mix well.

3. In a separate large bowl combine flour, spices, baking soda, and salt. Make a well in the center and pour in pumpkin mixture. Stir just until combined. Stir in cranberries and nuts, if using.

4. Spoon batter into 2 greased and floured 8x3¾x2½-inch loaf pans.

5. Bake in preheated oven for 1 hour, or until tester comes out clean. Makes 2 loaves. (Alternatively, use individual loaf pans. Reduce baking time.)

breakfast muffins

A filling and wholesome addition to your breakfast repertoire.

¾   cup oil

1½ cups brown sugar

1   teaspoon vanilla extract

2   eggs

2   cups water or milk

1   cup whole wheat flour

1½ cups flour

2   cups bran

1   teaspoon salt

2   teaspoons baking soda

1   cup raisins or chopped dates

½   cup chopped walnuts (optional)

1. Preheat oven to 350 degrees.

2. Mix oil, brown sugar, and vanilla in a large bowl.

3. Add eggs and water or milk; mix well.

4. Add dry ingredients, stirring until moistened.

5. Add raisins or dates and nuts, if using.

6. Pour batter into greased muffin tins. Bake in preheated oven for 20-25 minutes until tester comes out clean.

mujaddara

Mujaddara is equally tasty whether served hot or cold, which makes it a year-round favorite.

1½ cups brown lentils

1 cup rice (basmati or long-grain)

6 tablespoons olive oil

2½ cups thinly sliced onions

2½ cups water

Salt and freshly ground pepper, to taste

1. Rinse and sort lentils.

2. Rinse rice until water is almost clear, drain well.

3. Heat olive oil in a skillet until oil shimmers. Add onions and cook until deep brown, stirring often. Set onions aside to cool.

4. In a medium pot, combine lentils and water; simmer for 10 minutes.

5. Stir in rice, cover pot, and continue cooking for an additional 8-10 minutes until water is absorbed and rice and lentils are tender. Remove from heat and set aside for 5 minutes.

6. Mix lentils and rice with half of the onions. Cover and let stand for an additional 10 minutes. Season to taste with salt and pepper.

7. Serve topped with remaining onions.

classic stuffing *with* quinoa

A unique alternative to traditional bread stuffing.

2 cups chopped celery

1 clove garlic, chopped

1 medium onion, chopped

1 cup sliced mushrooms (optional)

2 tablespoons olive oil

2 cups quinoa, cooked

3 cups chicken, vegetable stock or water

2 tablespoons sage

2 tablespoons thyme

   Salt and pepper, to taste

1. Sauté celery, garlic, onion, and mushrooms (if using) in olive oil until onions are translucent.

2. Stir in quinoa until combined.

3. Add broth or water, herbs, salt, and pepper. Cover and simmer 15 minutes until quinoa is fully cooked.

4. Let stand covered for 5 minutes. Fluff with a fork before serving.

pullao rice *with* peas

The coconut milk and spices create a flavorful parve side dish.

1   cup basmati rice

1   tablespoon oil

½   small onion, diced

1¼ cups water

½   cup coconut milk

5   cardamom pods

1   teaspoon salt

1   pinch saffron or ¼ teaspoon turmeric powder

½   cup green peas (may be frozen)

1. Rinse rice well until water is almost clear.

2. Heat oil in a medium-sized pot and add onion. Reduce heat to medium-low and cook onions until translucent and softened.

3. Add rice and stir until rice is glistening.

4. Add water, coconut milk, cardamom, salt, and saffron or turmeric. Bring to a boil, cover, and reduce to low heat. Cook for approximately 7 minutes, and then add peas.

5. Continue cooking for an additional 3-5 minutes until liquid is absorbed and rice is tender.

6. Remove rice from heat and let stand covered for 5 minutes. Fluff gently with a fork before serving.

wheat berry salad

Wheat berries are an incredibly versatile fiber-rich grain. This dish keeps well overnight and can be served at room temperature, which considerably expands your serving options.

1½ cups wheat berries

4 cups water

1 cup chopped pecans

1 cup chopped dried currants, dried apricots, or golden raisins

½ cup chopped scallions (optional)

4 tablespoons parsley

2 tablespoons olive oil

Zest and juice of 1 orange

Salt and pepper, to taste

1. Simmer wheat berries in water for 60-90 minutes. Wheat berries will be firm but tender when cooked. (To shorten cooking time, soak wheat berries overnight, drain, and cook in fresh water.)

2. Drain wheat berries and mix with remaining ingredients while still hot.

3. Can be served warm or chilled.

whole wheat couscous *with* butternut squash, shallots, *and* figs

PARVE

This fragrant dish will satisfy sweet and savory palates alike.

1   butternut squash (2 pounds), peeled, seeded, and cut into 1-inch chunks

2   tablespoons olive oil

2   shallots, diced

1   teaspoon kosher salt

2   cloves garlic, finely chopped

⅛   teaspoon ground cinnamon

⅛   teaspoon ground nutmeg

1   teaspoon ground cumin, divided

12 dried figs, sliced

1½ cups water

1½ cups uncooked whole-wheat couscous

1. Preheat oven to 350 degrees.

2. Heat oil in a frying pan over medium heat.

3. Add shallots and salt; cook for 5 minutes.

4. Add garlic, cinnamon, nutmeg, and ½ teaspoon of the cumin; cook for 1 minute.

5. Add spice mixture to squash, tossing to coat. Place squash on baking sheet and roast in preheated oven for 15-20 minutes until squash is cooked through but still slightly firm.

6. Meanwhile, in a medium saucepan, bring 1½ cups water to a boil. Add the remaining cumin and a pinch salt to the water.

7. Stir in couscous. Cover, remove from heat, and let stand for 5-10 minutes. Fluff with a fork.

8. Add squash mixture to couscous.

9. Add figs and mix gently. Adjust salt and spices to taste.

persian orange rice

Citrus and cardamom complement each other in this long-grain rice dish.

2   cups basmati or Persian rice

3   oranges

3   cups water, approximately

3   tablespoons oil

4-5 pods cardamom

1   teaspoon salt

¼   cup sugar

1. Rinse rice under cool water until water is almost clear. Drain and set aside.

2. Wash and dry 2 of the oranges. Carefully peel rind from orange in long strips, without including the white pith. If necessary scrape white pith from rind. Stack strips and cut into long thin slivers.

3. Juice skinned oranges and remaining orange. Measure and add enough water to equal 3½ cups total.

4. Heat oil in a heavy-bottomed pan. Add drained rice and stir until rice is coated with oil and fragrant.

5. Add cardamom and slivered orange peels. Stir until well coated.

6. Add water, juice, salt, and sugar. Cover pot with a tight-fitting lid. Increase heat and bring rice to boil. Boil for 1 minute.

7. Reduce heat to low. Cook rice for 11 minutes, or until liquid has been absorbed.

8. Remove rice from heat and let stand for 5 minutes. Fluff rice gently with a fork.

sweet couscous pilaf

The almond milk gives this pilaf a creamy flavor that elevates the whole dish.

1½ cups whole-wheat couscous

3   cups almond milk, divided

½   cup sugar

⅓   cup dried cranberries, raisins, or chopped apricots

½   teaspoon salt

⅓   cup pine nuts, pistachios, cashews, or slivered almonds (toasted, if desired)

3   tablespoons butter or oil

2   carrots, shredded (optional)

1. Place couscous in a large microwavable bowl. Add 2 cups almond milk, stir, and let stand 15 minutes until most of the liquid has been absorbed.

2. Add remaining cup almond milk, sugar, cranberries, salt, nuts, oil or butter, and carrots (if using).

3. Cover bowl and microwave on high for 4-8 minutes, or until liquid has been absorbed.

4. Let stand covered for 2-3 minutes.

5. Mix couscous and fluff with a fork. May be served hot or at room temperature.

pasta liguria

DAIRY OR PARVE

Homemade croutons add crunch to this pasta dish.

2 cups whole wheat or multigrain bread, cut into ½-inch cubes

1 package (12-16 ounce) whole-wheat curly pasta, such as rotini or rotelle

3-4 tablespoons olive oil (plus additional for dressing pasta)

2-4 cloves garlic (depending on size and preference), peeled and minced

½ cup golden raisins

½ cup dark raisins

¼ cup pine nuts

¼ teaspoon crushed red pepper flakes

⅓ cup chopped flat-leaf parsley

Salt and freshly ground pepper, to taste

Freshly grated Parmesan cheese for serving (optional)

1. Preheat oven to 350 degrees.

2. Place bread cubes on a baking sheet. Bake in preheated oven approximately 10 minutes, or until golden brown, stirring or shaking once or twice.

3. Remove from oven and allow croutons to cool.

4. Bring a large pot of salted water to boil and cook pasta until tender. Drain well and place in a serving bowl.

5. While pasta cooks, heat 2-3 tablespoons of the oil in a large skillet (adding more as needed). Add minced garlic, raisins, pine nuts, and red pepper flakes; sauté until garlic and pine nuts begin to brown. Be careful not to let garlic and pine nuts burn.

6. Quickly add oil mixture to the hot pasta. Mix in parsley, salt, pepper, and croutons. Add more oil if pasta seems dry.

7. Adjust seasonings to taste. Sprinkle with Parmesan cheese, if using.

easy risotto

Risotto has a reputation for being difficult to create at home, but here is a simple recipe with impressive results and numerous variations.

5   cups low-sodium chicken or vegetable broth

1½ cups water

2   tablespoons unsalted olive oil or butter

1   medium leek or 1 small onion, finely chopped

¾   teaspoon salt

3   large cloves garlic, minced

2   cups Arborio rice

1   cup dry white wine

2   ounces grated Parmesan cheese
    (about 1 cup–dairy version)

1. Bring broth and water to a boil in large saucepan over high heat.

2. Reduce heat and maintain gentle simmer.

3. Heat oil or butter in large Dutch oven over medium heat; add leek or onion and salt. Cook, stirring frequently, 4-5 minutes until leek or onion is softened but not browned.

4. Add garlic and stir about 30 seconds until fragrant.

5. Add rice and cook, stirring frequently, about 3 minutes until grains are translucent around edges.

6. Add wine and cook, stirring constantly, 2-3 minutes until liquid is fully absorbed.

7. Stir 1 cup of the warm broth into rice and reduce heat to medium-low. Continue to stir until almost all liquid has been absorbed and rice is just al dente.

8. Add the next cup and repeat the process until all the broth is absorbed. Do not cover. The entire process should take about 18-20 minutes. Stir gently and constantly about 3 minutes until risotto becomes creamy.

9. If desired, add up to ½ cup additional broth to loosen texture of risotto. Serve immediately.

10. For dairy version, stir in Parmesan cheese and let stand 5 minutes before serving.

Variations:

spinach and herbs: *1 pound fresh spinach, chopped and steamed, or 1 package (10 ounce) frozen chopped spinach, thawed; 1 tablespoon fresh lemon juice; 2 tablespoons chopped parsley; 2 tablespoons chopped herbs (chives, dill, or thyme, or combination); salt and pepper. Add spinach at step 8 and heat until warmed thoroughly and creamy. Stir in remaining ingredients just before serving.*

asparagus: *4-6 spears asparagus, cut into 1½-inch pieces; 2 tablespoons chopped dill; 1 teaspoon tarragon (optional); 1 tablespoon chives (optional); juice of ½ lemon; salt and pepper. Add asparagus at step 8 and continue cooking until asparagus is tender and rice is creamy. Stir in herbs, lemon juice, and seasoning just before serving.*

chicken and mushroom: *2 bone-in chicken breasts; 1 cup chicken broth; 1 cup sliced mushrooms; 1 tablespoon sherry or brandy (optional); 1 tablespoon fresh lemon juice; 2 tablespoons chopped parsley; salt and papper. Season chicken breasts with salt and pepper and brown chicken in an oiled pan over high heat. Remove chicken and transfer to a small pot with chicken broth. Cover pot and simmer chicken 15-20 minutes until moist and tender. Let chicken cool in broth until easily handled. Remove skin and bones; shred chicken into bite-size pieces. While chicken is cooling, sauté sliced mushrooms in the same pan used to brown chicken. Cook until mushrooms have given up their liquid and are slightly browned. Add 1 tablespoon brandy or sherry, if desired, and cook until most of the liquid has boiled off. Stir in shredded chicken and adjust seasonings. Add mushrooms and chicken mixture to risotto at step 8. Stir in lemon juice and parsley just before serving.*

vegetable "bolognese" pasta

DAIRY

Finely chopped mushrooms stand in for ground meat in this delicious recipe.

1   ounce (28 g) dried porcini mushrooms (1 cup)

1   cup hot water

2   medium carrots, quartered lengthwise, then cut into 1-inch pieces

2   celery ribs, cut into 1-inch pieces

3   medium shallots, quartered lengthwise

1   medium red bell pepper, cut into 1-inch pieces

3   tablespoons olive oil

2   teaspoons chopped fresh rosemary

¾   teaspoon salt

½   teaspoon black pepper

2   tablespoons tomato paste

½   cup dry red wine

¾   pound uncooked pappardelle or wide linguine

½   cup finely grated Parmigiano-Reggiano cheese, plus additional for serving

1. Soak mushrooms in hot water 15 minutes.

2. Pulse carrots, celery, shallots, and bell pepper together in a food processor until coarsely chopped.

3. Heat oil in a 12-inch heavy skillet and sauté chopped vegetables, rosemary, salt, and pepper about 12 minutes until vegetables are golden brown and tender.

4. Lift reconstituted mushrooms out of soaking liquid, and squeeze excess liquid back into bowl (reserve liquid); rinse mushrooms well to remove any grit.

5. Finely chop mushrooms and add to vegetables in skillet. Stir in tomato paste and cook over moderate heat, stirring, 1 minute.

6. Add wine and raise heat to boil about 2 minutes until wine is reduced by about half.

7. Reduce heat to simmer.

8. Strain reserved mushroom-soaking liquid through a coffee filter or several layers of paper towels. Stir mushroom-soaking liquid and rosemary into sauce. Continue simmering until sauce is thick and fragrant.

9. While sauce is cooking, boil pasta in salted water until al dente.

10. Remove 1 cup of the pasta-cooking water, and then drain pasta in a colander.

11. Add pasta and ½ cup reserved cooking water to sauce, tossing to coat (thin sauce with additional cooking water if necessary).

12. Stir in cheese and serve immediately.

secret mac and cheese

A great way to get the kids to eat their veggies - and you too!

DAIRY

1   pound pasta shapes

1   small bunch broccoli, cut into florets (optional)

1   small head cauliflower, cut into florets (optional)

5   tablespoons butter or oil

1   small onion, chopped

1   clove garlic, minced

2   carrots, chopped (optional)

6   tablespoons flour

1½ teaspoons dry mustard (or 1 teaspoon Dijon mustard)

    Pinch cayenne pepper (optional)

4½ cups milk

2   cups shredded Monterey Jack cheese (Emek, mozzarella, or Muenster may be substituted), divided

2   cups shredded Cheddar cheese, divided

½   cup peas (optional)

½   cup corn (optional)

10 ounces spinach, frozen or fresh, cooked and squeezed dry (optional)

topping options: *(choose one)*

Seasoned breadcrumb topping, seasoned corn flake crumb topping, or crushed cracker topping (see recipes on next page)

1. Cook pasta in salted water until tender. Add broccoli or cauliflower (if using) to pasta approximately 5 minutes before finished. Drain pasta and vegetables, and set aside until needed.

2. In a heavy pot, heat butter until melted and foaming. Add onion and garlic and cook until softened. Stir in carrots, if using. Cook a few minutes until carrots begin to soften.

3. Add flour and cook roux until just beginning to color. Stir in dry mustard and cayenne. Add milk, whisking to incorporate. Bring sauce to a boil, whisking or stirring constantly. Reduce heat and simmer sauce for approximately 3 minutes until sauce is consistency of thick cream.

4. Preheat oven to 350 degrees.

5. Remove sauce from heat and stir in half of the cheese. Mix in vegetables and pasta, stirring well to combine. Season to taste with salt and pepper.

6. Place half of the pasta mixture in an oiled baking dish. Sprinkle with remaining cheese. Top with remaining pasta. Sprinkle with choice of topping.

7. Bake in preheated oven approximately 30-45 minutes until heated through. If using breadcrumb topping, brown casserole under broiler about 3 minutes until browned and bubbly.

topping options:

seasoned breadcrumbs:

½ cup panko or fresh breadcrumbs

1-2 tablespoons Parmesan cheese

1 tablespoon oil

1 tablespoon herbs

Salt and pepper, to taste

1. Combine breadcrumbs with Parmesan cheese, oil, and herbs.
2. Season with salt and pepper to taste.

seasoned corn flake crumbs:

1 cup crushed corn flakes

2 teaspoons dried herbs

Salt and pepper, to taste

1. Combine corn flake crumbs with Parmesan cheese, dried herbs, salt, and pepper.

crushed crackers:

1 cup crushed crackers

winter green lasagna

DAIRY

For those lasagna lovers who prefer less sauce and more vegetables. The no-boil noodles lower prep time and the dirty-pot quotient.

2½ pounds fresh kale, Swiss chard, spinach, or another fresh green, or 5 (10 ounce) boxes frozen chopped spinach, thawed

4   tablespoons olive oil, divided

2   garlic cloves, minced

1   teaspoon kosher salt, divided

2   tablespoons all-purpose flour

3   cups low-fat milk

2   cups freshly grated Parmesan, Romano, or a combination, divided

2   containers (15 ounce) ricotta

2   eggs, beaten

½   teaspoon ground nutmeg

1   box (16 ounce) no-boil lasagna noodles

Zest of 1 lemon, grated

1. If using fresh greens, discard any tough stems and chop leaves. Rinse well and shake gently to remove most but not all of the water.

2. Place 2 tablespoons of the oil in a large saucepan with garlic and cook over medium-high heat until garlic begins to brown.

3. Add greens and toss. Add ½ teaspoon of the salt.

4. Cover immediately and cook over medium heat, stirring occasionally, for 10 minutes, or until greens are wilted and tender. (If using frozen spinach, press out liquid, then sauté spinach in 2 tablespoons of the oil and garlic for about 5 minutes.)

5. Transfer greens to a bowl and set aside to cool. Discard any accumulated juices.

6. In the same pot, heat remaining 2 tablespoons oil over medium heat. Add flour and remaining ½ teaspoon salt and cook roux, whisking constantly, for about 3 minutes.

7. Add milk and increase heat to medium-high. Cook, stirring constantly, about 10 minutes until sauce thickens and boils.

8. Reduce heat and stir in 1½ cups of the grated cheese.

9. Preheat oven to 350 degrees.

10. Coat a 13x9-inch baking pan with cooking spray.

11. Blend ricotta, eggs, lemon zest, and nutmeg into the greens.

12. Spread about ½ cup of the cheese sauce in the bottom of the baking pan. Place 3 sheets of pasta on top. Spread ¼ of the spinach filling and ½ cup of the cheese sauce, then another 3 sheets of pasta. Make 3 more layers. End with pasta and sauce; sprinkle with the remaining ½ cup cheese.

13. Cover with foil and bake 45 minutes. Remove the foil and cook 15 minutes more, or until golden.

14. Let stand 10 minutes before serving.

Hint: *Lasagna can be made up to 1 day ahead. Cover and refrigerate. Reheat in a 325 degree oven for 20 minutes, or until a knife inserted in the center comes out hot.*

mediterranean quinoa

DAIRY

The versatility of this summery grain dish is limited only by your creativity.

1½ cups quinoa, uncooked

3-4 cups water or vegetable broth

¼ cup apple cider vinegar

Juice of 1 lemon

2 cloves garlic, minced

3 tablespoons olive oil

⅓ cup chopped fresh parsley

½ cup sliced kalamata olives (optional)

1 red onion, diced

1 cup cherry tomatoes, sliced in half

½ cup chopped artichoke hearts (optional)

Salt and pepper, to taste

½ cup crumbled feta cheese

Steamed broccoli florets; steamed snap peas; diced red, yellow, or green peppers (optional additions)

1. In a medium-large covered saucepan, cook quinoa in water or vegetable broth for 15-20 minutes until tender, stirring occasionally.

2. Remove from heat and set quinoa aside to cool.

3. In a small bowl, whisk together vinegar, lemon juice, garlic, and olive oil.

4. Gently toss quinoa together with parsley, olives, onion, tomatoes, artichokes, and optional additions, if using.

5. Pour olive oil mixture over quinoa. Season to taste with salt and pepper; gently stir in feta cheese.

6. Serve room temperature or chilled.

penne with sausage, baby spinach, and tomatoes

MEAT

An Italian classic that is a super-satisfying main course.

2 tablespoons extra-virgin olive oil

1 pound sweet or hot Italian sausage, cut into 1-inch pieces

1 red bell pepper, cut into ½-inch pieces

3 large cloves garlic, thinly sliced lengthwise

½ cup dry white wine

1 can (28-32 ounce) whole tomatoes in juice

¼ teaspoon black pepper

2 cups baby spinach leaves

1 pound penne

Salt and pepper, to taste

1. Heat oil in a 12-inch heavy skillet over moderately high heat; add sausage and cook, stirring, 5-7 minutes until sausage is browned.

2. Transfer meat to a bowl using a slotted spoon. Add bell pepper and garlic to fat in skillet. Reduce heat to moderate and cook, stirring occasionally, 5-6 minutes until pepper is just tender and garlic is golden.

3. Add cooked sausage to the pan along with wine. Increase heat and stir, scraping up brown bits on bottom of skillet with a wooden spoon. Continue cooking about 2 minutes until liquid is reduced by half.

4. Add tomatoes with juice and black pepper; simmer, breaking up tomatoes with spoon, 6-8 minutes until sauce is slightly thickened.

5. Add spinach and mix thoroughly. Continue cooking until spinach is wilted.

6. While sauce is cooking, cook pasta in a 6-8-quart pot of boiling salted water until al dente. Reserve ½ cup pasta cooking water, then drain pasta in a colander and return to pot.

7. Add sauce to pasta and toss to coat. Add cooking water if necessary to moisten. Season to taste with salt and pepper.

pasta caprese

Marinating the tomatoes is the secret to the deep flavors of this dish.

1   pound ripe tomatoes

4   cloves garlic, chopped

½   cup coarsely chopped fresh basil

⅓   cup olive oil

1   teaspoon salt

1   teaspoon pepper

1   pound linguine or spaghetti

2   tablespoons pine nuts (optional)

1. Core and chop tomatoes. Transfer tomatoes along with juices to a nonreactive bowl.

2. Stir in garlic, basil, olive oil, salt, and pepper. Cover and let tomato mixture marinate at room temperature at least 45 minutes and up to 6 hours. (May be stored in refrigerator overnight — bring to room temperature before using.)

3. Cook pasta in salted water until al dente.

4. Drain pasta and transfer to a large bowl. Add marinated tomatoes and toss until mixed well. Let pasta stand 10-15 minutes to allow flavors to meld.

5. Toss with pine nuts, if using.

6. Serve at room temperature or slightly chilled.

Variations:

1. Toss pasta with sliced roasted zucchini, broccoli, or eggplant before adding marinated tomatoes.

2. Toss pasta with 2-3 tablespoons drained capers just before serving.

meat lasagna

Use the meat sauce in this crowd-pleasing lasagna to add heartiness to any pasta dish.

breadcrumbs:

½ cup fresh breadcrumbs or panko

1 tablespoon oil

1 teaspoon crushed garlic

1 tablespoon chopped herbs

Salt and pepper, to taste

lasagna:

3 tablespoons olive oil

1 onion, chopped

3 tablespoons chopped garlic

1 small carrot, coarsely chopped (optional)

1½ pounds ground beef
(or mixture of ground veal and beef)

1 pound sausage, thinly sliced or chopped
(optional)

1 cup fruity white wine
(white zinfandel works especially well)

1 can (28 ounce) chopped tomatoes

1 can (16 ounce) crushed tomatoes

2 tablespoons tomato paste (optional)

2 tablespoons chopped parsley

1 tablespoon each minced fresh oregano and
thyme
(or 1 teaspoon dried oregano and thyme)

2 tablespoons chopped fresh basil
(or 1 teaspoon dried basil)

Salt and pepper, to taste

½ pound lasagna noodles, boiled until just
softened

Olive oil for pan

1. Mix breadcrumbs or panko with oil, garlic, herbs, salt, and pepper. Set aside.

2. To prepare sauce, heat oil in a large wide pan and sauté onion, garlic, and chopped carrot until softened and fragrant.

3. Add ground beef, gently breaking into large pieces with a spoon. Cook slightly; meat should still be pink.

4. Add sausages and cook until browned and heated through.

5. Add wine, adjusting heat so wine is simmering. Cook meat until wine has almost completely evaporated, breaking up meat with a spoon. Meat will still be somewhat chunky.

6. Add chopped tomatoes with juice and crushed tomatoes. Stir in tomato paste and dried herbs, if using. Continue simmering sauce, uncovered, approximately 15-20 minutes until thickened.

7. Stir in fresh herbs. Season to taste with salt and pepper.

8. Preheat oven to 375 degrees.

9. To assemble lasagna, oil a large baking dish and spread ½ cup sauce on bottom of dish. Place lasagna noodles in a single layer on top of sauce. Spread ⅓ of the remaining sauce on top of noodles. Place another layer of noodles on top. Spread another ⅓ of the sauce and another layer of noodles. Top with remaining sauce. Sprinkle top with breadcrumb mixture. Bake on a tray for 30 minutes, or until lasagna is bubbling and topping is lightly browned.

fish

fish

wild salmon *with* french green lentils

PARVE

A gorgeous dish packed with flavor and color.

6 (4 ounce) wild Alaskan salmon fillets, with skin

Peanut oil for frying

Salt and pepper, to taste

1 Vidalia onion, finely diced

1 small carrot, peeled and finely diced

1 stalk celery, finely diced

½ bulb fennel, finely diced

Extra-virgin olive oil

1 box (17 ounce) French green lentils

3 tablespoons chopped flat-leaf parsley

2 tablespoons chopped tarragon leaves

vinaigrette:

1 shallot, minced

4 tablespoons whole grain mustard

2 tablespoons red wine vinegar

1 tablespoon honey

6 tablespoons extra-virgin olive oil

Salt and pepper, to taste

1. Using a sharp knife, make three parallel cuts just through the skin of the fish, being careful not to cut too deeply. This will prevent fish from curling up in the pan during cooking.

2. Preheat oven to 400 degrees.

3. Heat a non-stick, ovenproof skillet with just enough peanut oil to cover the bottom of the pan.

4. Season fish on both sides with salt and pepper; add fish to the pan, skin side down. With the flame on medium high, cook fish about 4 minutes until the skin crisps up. Place the pan in preheated oven for another 4 minutes until fish is barely cooked through. Remove from oven and tent loosely to keep warm.

5. In a large shallow pan, sauté onion, carrots, celery, and fennel in olive oil until softened.

6. Add lentils and sauté with vegetables for 1 minute more. This will allow lentils to be fully coated with oil. Season to taste with salt and pepper.

7. Add enough water to cover lentils. Bring the pot to a simmer and continue cooking on low heat until all of the water is absorbed and lentils are tender.

8. If serving immediately, gently fold herbs into lentils and transfer to a serving platter. If serving later, allow lentils to cool. Reheat on low heat before folding in herbs and serving.

9. To prepare vinaigrette, whisk together mustard, vinegar, honey, and shallots. Pour in olive oil in a slow stream while whisking vigorously. Season to taste with salt and pepper.

10. To serve, place warm lentils on the plate and top with salmon, skin side up. Drizzle a small amount of the vinaigrette onto the plate.

fiery fish tacos

These tacos make for a fun dinner, where family members can choose their favorite vegetables and condiments to suit their tastes.

6   (4 ounce) fresh tilapia or firm white fish fillets, skinned and boned

1-2 teaspoons cayenne pepper

Juice of 2 limes, divided

1   fresh ear of corn, cooked, removing and keeping only kernels

½   cup finely diced red onion

½   cup finely diced jicama (optional)

½   cup finely diced red bell pepper

½   cup finely chopped cilantro

Zest of 1 lime

⅓   cup sour cream

1-2 teaspoons cayenne pepper or chipotle, to taste

2   tablespoons olive oil

Salt and pepper, to taste

8   (5-inch) flour tortillas

1. Rinse fish fillets and pat dry. Place fish in a zip-top bag.

2. Mix together cayenne pepper and 2 tablespoons of the lime juice and pour over fish. Seal bag and marinate refrigerated for 1-2 hours, or at room temperature for 20 minutes.

3. In a medium bowl, mix together corn, red onion, jicama, red bell pepper, and cilantro. Stir in juice from 1 lime.

4. In a small bowl, mix together sour cream, remaining lime juice, and 1-2 teaspoons cayenne pepper.

5. Heat oil in a large frying pan. Sear fillets on both sides until they are just cooked through, then lower the heat and flake fish off into tiny pieces and continue to heat for another 1-2 minutes. Be sure not to overcook and dry out fish.

6. Add salt and pepper.

7. Tortillas can be either warmed in an oven or warmed in an ungreased frying pan over medium-high heat.

8. To serve, spread sour cream mixture on each tortilla; then top with corn salsa and flaked fish. Carefully fold tortilla in thirds over filling.

brook trout with shallots, roasted fennel, and tomatoes

The bold punch of the shallots, fennel, and tomatoes elevates the mild flavor of the trout or any white fish.

10-12 cherry tomatoes

4 tablespoons olive oil, divided

Salt and pepper

1 teaspoon fresh chopped rosemary

2 small fennel bulbs, thinly sliced

3 shallots, sliced thin

4 trout fillets (or any other mild white fish) at least ½-inch thick

½ cup dry white wine

Fresh minced parsley

1. Preheat oven to 400 degrees.

2. Fit a sheet pan with parchment paper or aluminum foil.

3. Toss tomatoes with 1 tablespoon olive oil, salt, pepper, and chopped rosemary; place on sheet pan.

4. Scatter sliced fennel on the same sheet pan and toss with ½ tablespoon olive oil, salt, and pepper. Spread vegetables to single layer.

5. Roast for about 15 minutes until tomatoes burst open.

6. While vegetables are roasting, sauté shallots in a pan with 1 tablespoon olive oil until softened. Remove shallots from pan and set aside.

7. Season fish to taste with salt and pepper. Add remaining olive oil to pan, and heat over medium flame until oil shimmers. Place fish skin side up in pan and sauté without moving fish for 3-4 minutes. Flip over carefully and sauté another 2 minutes, depending on thickness of fish (if thinner, cook less; if thicker, cook more).

8. Pour in wine and boil to reduce by half. When reduced, add a small amount of olive oil and stir.

9. Add fresh chopped parsley, salt, and pepper to taste.

10. To serve, remove fish from pan and place on a plate. Spread out shallots over fish and place roasted tomatoes and fennel over fish as well. Pour wine sauce over fish and veggies, and top with more chopped parsley.

sea bass kabobs

PARVE

Using this recipe, you can incorporate fish as a finger food.

¼   cup tamari or soy sauce

¼   cup honey

1   tablespoon rice vinegar

1   teaspoon minced ginger

1   clove garlic, minced

1½   pounds sea bass, skinned, boned, and cut into 1-inch cubes

1   red pepper, cut into ¾-inch pieces

1   onion, cut into ¾-inch pieces

8-12 wooden skewers

1. Combine soy sauce, honey, vinegar, ginger, and garlic; mix well.

2. Place fish, peppers, and onion into zip-top bag; cover with marinade. Marinate in the refrigerator for 2-6 hours.

3. Soak wood skewers in water for 10-15 minutes. This will help prevent burning when placed on the grill or under the broiler.

4. Thread skewers with bass, onion, and pepper in an alternating pattern, leaving the last inch of skewer empty.

5. Grill on barbecue at medium-high heat for about 15 minutes, checking often. Alternately, broil skewers for approximately 15 minutes.

Variation: Use salmon and sea bass to make a 2-fish kabob. Use only ¾ pound of sea bass and add ¾ pound salmon.

Note: Fish pieces should be large enough so that they don't break when skewering; it is important that all pieces are the same size so that they cook evenly.

tea-poached cod *with* zucchini sauté

PARVE

An unusual cooking method that infuses the cod with a subtle flavor that works really well with the zucchini sauté.

poaching:

8   (4 ounce) fillets of skinless fresh cod, room
      temperature

      Salt and pepper, to taste

10   thyme sprigs, separated

6   cups water

1   cup dry white wine

2   green tea bags

1   orange, quartered

2   cloves garlic

zucchini sauté:

3   tablespoons extra-virgin olive oil

2   cups sliced onions

2   cloves garlic, sliced

1   small zucchini, sliced into half moons

3   ripe tomatoes, diced

1   cup sliced black olives

2   tablespoons capers

2   tablespoons freshly chopped thyme leaves

2   tablespoons freshly chopped flat-leaf parsley

      Salt and pepper, to taste

1. Place cod fillets in a dish that is at least the same depth as the fish fillets. Season fish with salt and pepper.

2. Place 5 of the thyme sprigs in the dish next to fillets.

3. In a large saucepan, add water, wine, tea bags, orange, garlic, remaining 5 thyme sprigs, and salt and pepper. Bring to a boil and then simmer for about 10 minutes.

4. Strain liquid directly over cod fillets, making sure fillets are completely covered in the liquid. Leave cod in liquid at room temperature for about 12 minutes. At this point the fish should be perfectly poached. If not serving right away, refrigerate fish in poaching liquid.

5. For the sauce: Heat olive oil in a large pan, add onions, and sauté approximately 6 minutes until softened.

6. Add sliced garlic cloves and sauté for 2 more minutes.

7. Add zucchini, tomatoes, olives, and capers. Let cook for about 5 minutes until vegetables soften and release some of their juices.

8. Add herbs; season to taste with salt and pepper.

9. Remove cod from poaching liquid and top with vegetables. If not serving immediately, the dish can be refrigerated for up to 2 days and then reheated or served cold.

Note: If cod doesn't appear to be poached within the given time, place fish with poaching liquid into a preheated 300-degree oven for 10 minutes.

simple smoked salmon family-style

Grilling the salmon outside takes the heat out of your kitchen in those hot summer months.

1   Alder or cedar wood grilling plank per salmon fillet

1   (3 pound) salmon fillet, with skin

dry rub:

1   tablespoon coarse sea salt

1½ tablespoons brown sugar

1   tablespoon cracked black pepper

1   teaspoon garlic powder

1   teaspoon onion powder

½   teaspoon cayenne pepper

1   teaspoon mustard seeds (optional)

1. Soak wood plank in water for at least 30 minutes.

2. Preheat gas grill to medium-low heat (about 160-180 degrees).

3. To prepare dry rub, combine sea salt, brown sugar, black pepper, garlic powder, onion powder, cayenne pepper, and mustard seeds.

4. Place salmon, skin side down, on soaked plank and work in dry rub.

5. Place plank in a covered grill and smoke for at least 2 hours, checking after 1½ hours for doneness. Fish is done when it flakes with a fork, and it should not be too salty. As fish smokes, the salt content reduces. Adjust the cooking time and salt to your taste.

Note: Smoking fish can take between 2-6 hours, depending on personal taste, the size of the fillet, and the fat content of the fish.

asian seafood sliders

Move over, gefilte fish; there is a new appetizer in town.

burgers:

1½ pounds fresh salmon or tuna, boned, skinned, and cubed into 2-inch chunks

¼ cup chopped scallion including greens

2 teaspoons minced ginger

3 cloves garlic, minced

2 tablespoons tamari or soy sauce

2-3 tablespoons sesame oil

3 tablespoons chopped parsley

2 tablespoons brown sugar (white sugar or ½ tablespoon honey can be substituted)

Juice of 1 lime

Grated rind from 1 lime (optional)

1-2 teaspoons fresh chili pepper (optional)

Salt and pepper, to taste

Oil for frying

Rolls or buns for sliders

spicy mayo:

1 clove garlic, minced

½ teaspoon sea salt

2 teaspoons chili powder

⅛ teaspoon cayenne pepper

2 tablespoons fresh lime juice

½ cup light mayonnaise

avocado mayo:

1 large avocado

5 tablespoons light mayonnaise

1 tablespoon fresh lime juice

¾ teaspoon hot pepper sauce

1. Place all burger ingredients (except frying oil) in a food processor and pulse until fish is coarsely chopped. Be careful not to overprocess. Mixture should be quite chunky, but should hold together when formed into patties.

2. Form fish into patties approximately 1 inch thick and 2-3 inches in diameter. Patties can be made 1-2 hours ahead and stored in the refrigerator until ready to be cooked.

3. Heat oil in skillet, and place sliders in the skillet for 3 minutes per side until just cooked through.

4. To make spicy mayo, mix all ingredients together and chill.

5. To make avocado mayo, blend all ingredients in a food processor until smooth and chill.

6. Serve sliders with either spicy or avocado mayo, some mixed greens, and your favorite burger toppings on a lightly toasted bun.

baked honey-mustard red snapper

PARVE

A tantalizing no-fuss dish with little prep and cook time.

¾ cup spicy brown mustard

⅓ cup honey

1 tablespoon vinegar

2 cups panko breadcrumbs

Salt and pepper

6 red snapper fillets, ½ pound each
(tilapia or flounder may be substituted)

1. Preheat oven to 400 degrees.

2. In a bowl, combine mustard, honey, and vinegar.

3. In another bowl, season breadcrumbs with salt and pepper.

4. Cover both sides of fillets with honey-mustard combination, then coat each fillet with breadcrumbs. Bake for approximately 15-20 minutes until golden brown.

5. Turn broiler to low and broil fish directly under heat for an additional 3-5 minutes, until panko is lightly browned and crisped.

tuna ceviche

PARVE

Ceviche is a method of "cooking" fish by marinating it in citrus juices. In this version, the bright flavors of the marinade enhance the freshness of the tuna.

2 pounds sushi-grade tuna (salmon or other firm-fleshed fish), cut into ½-inch or smaller pieces

½ red onion, finely diced

1 cup chopped fresh seeded tomatoes

1 serrano chili, seeded and finely diced

2 teaspoons salt

Dash hot sauce

Dash ground oregano

½ cup fresh-squeezed lime juice

½ cup fresh-squeezed lemon juice

Pinch fresh cilantro

1 avocado, diced

Blue corn tortilla chips

1. Place tuna, onion, tomatoes, chili, salt, hot sauce, and oregano in a glass dish. Cover with lime juice and lemon juice. Let sit covered in refrigerator for 1 hour, then stir, making sure all the fish is exposed to the juices.

2. Let sit in refrigerator for 2-3 more hours, giving time for flavors to blend.

3. Before serving, add the diced avocado.

4. Serve with tortilla chips.

steamed sea bass *with* ginger *and* shiitakes

The pepper and chili-infused sesame oil add some heat and Asian flair to this steamed fish dish.

4 (6 ounce) sea bass fillets

Sea salt

Black pepper

Pinch cayenne pepper

¼ cup sliced fresh ginger

1 cup sliced shiitake mushrooms

2 tablespoons chopped fresh cilantro

2 tablespoons regular or chili-infused sesame oil

6 scallions cut into ½-inch pieces

1 tablespoon low-sodium soy sauce

Black sesame seeds (optional)

1. Bring water to boil under a metal or bamboo steamer.

2. Sprinkle sea bass with sea salt, black pepper, and cayenne pepper, then place on a piece of parchment paper inside a steamer. Top with ginger and shiitakes. Cover and steam 15 minutes.

3. Remove fish and mushrooms with a slotted spoon and place on a plate. Sprinkle cilantro on top and drizzle with juices from the parchment paper.

4. In a small sauté pan, heat oil over medium heat for 1-2 minutes, or until smoking. Remove from heat and immediately add scallions to oil for about a minute; remove scallions and add on top of fish. Pour some of the oil on top to wilt cilantro.

5. Drizzle soy sauce on top. Sprinkle with black sesame seeds (optional).

family-style halibut *with* black olive salsa

The contrast of the salsa on the delicate white fish is striking. As pretty as it is delicious.

3 tablespoons olive oil

Juice of 1 lemon

Salt and pepper

1½ pounds halibut fillets or steaks

black olive salsa:

1 cup pitted black olives

¾ cup chopped sun-dried tomatoes packed in oil

2 teaspoons chopped basil

2 teaspoons chopped dill

Juice of 1 lemon

½ chili, seeded and chopped

2 teaspoons olive oil

1. In a bowl mix olive oil, lemon juice, salt, and pepper, pour over fish, and marinate for about 20 minutes.

2. While fish is marinating, mix salsa ingredients and let stand at room temperature for 10-15 minutes.

3. Remove fish from marinade and pan-fry on medium-high heat in a lightly oiled pan about 8 minutes per side until cooked.

4. Serve fish topped with salsa.

glazed salmon

Adding the dried apricots to the apricot preserves creates a more interesting texture.

1   cup apricot preserves

⅓   cup finely chopped dried apricots

2   tablespoons soy sauce

1   tablespoon fresh grated ginger

2   cloves garlic, minced

¼   teaspoon cinnamon

4   skinless salmon fillets

1. Preheat broiler and grease a broiler pan.

2. In a saucepan over medium heat, mix together apricot preserves, dried apricots, soy sauce, ginger, garlic, and cinnamon. Bring to a boil, and then reduce heat to medium-low and simmer about 20 minutes until reduced by about half. Stir occasionally.

3. Remove ¼ cup of the glaze for basting and set the rest aside.

4. Place salmon in the greased broiler pan and brush with glaze. Broil 3 inches from the heat for a total of 8-12 minutes, or until salmon flakes easily with a fork.

5. After about 5 minutes, gently turn fish over and baste it with the reserved glaze.

6. During the last 2 minutes, baste again. Serve with reserved sauce.

poultry

roast chicken *with* parsley *and* onions

MEAT

Repeated bastings create a juicy, succulent finished product.

1 tablespoon fresh lemon juice

1¼ cups fresh parsley or chervil, minced, divided

1 tablespoon minced garlic

1 whole chicken (3-4 pounds)

3 tablespoons olive oil

2 cups sliced onions

½ cup chicken stock or water

1. Preheat oven to 400 degrees.

2. Combine lemon juice, ¼ cup of the parsley (or chervil) and garlic in bowl and rub mixture all over chicken. Place chicken, breast side down, on a rack in a roasting pan, and place in preheated oven.

3. Heat oil in a large skillet over medium heat; add onions and sauté for 10 minutes.

4. Stir stock (or water) and remaining parsley (or chervil) into onion mixture and simmer on low heat.

5. After chicken has roasted for 20 minutes, spread some of the onion mixture on top, then turn chicken breast side up and top with more of the onion mixture. Leave some of the onion mixture in the skillet for serving.

6. Cook chicken approximately 8 more minutes (or longer if breast is not yet browning), then baste with the pan juices.

7. Turn oven down to 325 degrees, baste again, and continue roasting approximately 1 hour until internal temperature of chicken reaches 160 degrees.

8. Pour pan juices into remaining onion mixture, reheat, and serve on the side.

tandoori chicken

MEAT

An economical dish that highlights Indian food's fragrant and rich qualities.

8   chicken legs or thighs, skin removed

1   teaspoon salt

     Juice of ½ large lemon

1   tablespoon chopped ginger

3-4 cloves garlic, chopped

2   teaspoons garam masala

½   teaspoon ground cumin

1   teaspoon chili powder (optional)

1. Make several shallow cuts in each piece of chicken with a sharp knife. Place chicken pieces in a gallon-size zip-top plastic bag. Add all other ingredients. Seal bag and gently shake to mix ingredients and coat chicken pieces. Marinate overnight in refrigerator.

2. Preheat oven to 400 degrees.

3. Remove chicken from marinade and place on a jelly-roll pan lightly coated with olive oil.

4. Cook in preheated oven for approximately 45 minutes to 1 hour until juices run clear.

oven fried chicken

A richly satisfying chicken recipe that has all the taste and crunch of fried chicken with almost none of the grease.

2 cups soy milk or rice milk mixed with 2 tablespoons vinegar, or 1½ cups soy yogurt thinned with ½ cup soy milk or water

2 tablespoons Dijon mustard

2 teaspoons salt

1 teaspoon black pepper

2 tablespoons minced garlic, divided

Hot sauce to taste

8 split bone-in chicken breasts, skinned (alternately, 2-3 pound bone-in chicken parts)

2½ cups crushed corn flakes

¾ cup breadcrumbs

½ teaspoon sage

½ teaspoon thyme

½ teaspoon oregano

½ teaspoon paprika

Cayenne pepper, to taste

¼ cup oil (olive oil, canola, or other mild oil)

1. Whisk soy milk mixture, mustard, salt, black pepper, 1 tablespoon of the minced garlic, and hot sauce together in a large bowl (or gallon-size zip-top bag).

2. Cover chicken with marinade. Refrigerate overnight or for a minimum of 1 hour.

3. Preheat oven to 400 degrees.

4. Line baking sheet with foil. Set a wire rack on the sheet so that chicken will become crisp on all sides.

5. Gently toss corn flakes, breadcrumbs, remaining garlic, black pepper, salt, sage, thyme, oregano, paprika, and cayenne pepper in a shallow dish until well combined.

6. Drizzle oil over crumbs and toss until well coated.

7. Working with one piece at a time, remove chicken from marinade and dredge in the crumb mixture, firmly pressing crumbs on all sides of chicken.

8. Place chicken on prepared rack, leaving ½ inch space between pieces.

9. Bake approximately 45 minutes in preheated oven until chicken is a deep golden brown.

paella

A complex Spanish-style one-pot meal.

1   whole chicken, cut into 8 or more pieces

Salt and pepper, to taste

Generous pinch saffron

⅓   cup white wine
(brandy or vermouth may be substituted)

3-4   tablespoons olive oil, divided

1   pound merguez or spicy sausage, cut into
1-inch pieces

1   pound mild sausage, cut into 1-inch pieces

½   pound turkey cubanos or smoked sausage,
cut into 1-inch pieces

1   onion, diced

1   tomato, chopped

1   red or yellow pepper, chopped

2   cups paella rice or Arborio rice

3-4   cloves garlic, minced

2   tablespoons smoked Spanish paprika
(if unavailable, regular paprika may be
substituted)

3   cups chicken stock

1   box frozen artichoke hearts, thawed

½-1 pound green beans or sugar snap peas

½   cup oil-cured, kalamata, or Israeli black olives
(optional)

1. Season chicken to taste with salt and pepper.
2. In a small cup or bowl, crush saffron and mix with white wine. Let stand for 5-10 minutes to allow saffron to infuse.
3. Heat 1-2 tablespoons olive oil in a large wide sauté pan or Dutch oven and brown chicken pieces. Remove chicken and set aside.
4. Add all sausages to the sauté pan and brown. Remove and set aside.
5. Add remaining olive oil to pan and sauté onion, tomato, garlic, and chopped pepper until well softened.
6. Rinse rice well and drain. Add to sautéing vegetables and stir to coat.
7. Stir in smoked paprika. Add saffron and white wine infusion, scraping up any browned bits. Reduce heat and add chicken stock.
8. Place chicken on top of vegetable/rice mixture. Add sausages, distributing evenly on top of chicken. Layer artichokes and green beans (or sugar snap peas) on top of sausages.
9. Bring broth to gentle simmer, cover pan, and cook gently 30-40 minutes until broth is absorbed. Shake pan every 10 minutes, to minimize sticking.
10. Preheat oven to 400 degrees.
11. Remove lid to check rice. If rice seems underdone, add more broth or water. Cover and continue cooking until broth is absorbed and rice is tender.
12. Sprinkle olives on top, if using.
13. Place covered pan in preheated oven for 10-20 minutes, to complete cooking.
14. Serve hot. Reheats well.

gaga chicken

A sure-fire crowd pleaser.

1   cup ketchup

1   cup honey

⅓   cup soy sauce

2   cloves garlic, chopped

1-2 tablespoons basil

1   tablespoon pepper

2   chickens cut into eight pieces each

1. Mix all ingredients (other than chicken) together. Divide sauce and pour into 2 gallon-size zip-top plastic bags.

2. Immerse chicken parts in sauce and marinate at least 1 hour or overnight, refrigerated.

3. Preheat oven to 375 degrees.

4. Line a pan (or two if needed) with 2 layers of heavy-duty foil.

5. Remove chicken from marinade and place chicken parts in pan(s), leaving space between pieces.

6. Bake for 45-60 minutes.

chicken with mushrooms and chives

This comforting chicken dish will conjure aromas of Italy.

sauce:

⅓ cup fresh squeezed lemon juice

⅓ cup light olive oil

¼ cup soy sauce

chicken:

1 chicken cut into 8 pieces

1 pound mushrooms, thinly sliced

2-3 tablespoons chopped chives, plus additional
    for serving

2-3 tablespoons chopped garlic

1. Preheat oven to 350 degrees.

2. In a bowl, whisk together all sauce ingredients.

3. Place chicken in well-greased shallow baking pan. Sprinkle mushrooms, chives, and garlic over chicken. Pour sauce over chicken.

4. Cover pan with foil and place in preheated oven for 20 minutes.

5. Remove chicken from oven, uncover, and baste with pan juices.

6. Return chicken to oven uncovered for another 10-20 minutes until chicken is baked through and golden brown.

7. Add fresh chopped chives before serving.

panko chicken fingers *with* apricot mustard dipping sauce

Crunchy chicken fingers with a tangy dipping sauce. A great weeknight dinner that will be loved by kids and grown-ups alike.

chicken:

½ cup all-purpose flour

   Coarse salt and freshly ground black pepper, to taste

2 large eggs

2 tablespoons water

1 tablespoon Dijon mustard

1½ cups panko breadcrumbs

2 tablespoons extra-virgin olive oil

   Pinch cayenne pepper

4 large boneless, skinless chicken breast halves (about 2 pounds), cut into strips

   Olive oil cooking spray

apricot mustard dipping sauce:

1 cup apricot jam or preserves

¼ cup Dijon mustard

1 teaspoon chopped fresh thyme leaves

1. Preheat oven to 375 degrees.

2. Line a baking sheet with parchment paper and spray with cooking spray; set aside.

3. Place flour in a large bowl and season very generously with salt and pepper.

4. Whisk eggs in another large bowl with water and Dijon mustard until well combined.

5. Place breadcrumbs in a third large bowl, and drizzle with olive oil; toss to coat. Stir in cayenne and mix well.

6. Place chicken pieces in seasoned flour, and toss to coat. Shake off any excess flour from chicken pieces and transfer chicken to egg mixture. Turn to coat chicken pieces.

7. Transfer coated chicken pieces to breadcrumb mixture and toss until completely coated. Place breaded chicken pieces on baking sheet. Spray generously with olive oil spray.

8. Bake in preheated oven until golden brown and chicken is cooked through, 18-20 minutes.

9. To prepare dipping sauce, combine apricot jam, mustard, and thyme together in a small bowl. Stir until well combined.

chicken braised with olives

Braising completely infuses the chicken with flavor and makes it so soft and juicy it will fall right off the bone.

¼ cup all-purpose flour

Salt and black pepper, to taste

1 whole chicken, cut in 8 pieces, skin removed, or any combination of bone-in chicken pieces

2 tablespoons olive oil, divided

1 large onion, chopped

4 cloves garlic, thinly sliced

1¼ cups chicken broth

2 tablespoons tomato paste

½ cup pitted and halved kalamata olives

1. Place flour on a plate; season with salt and pepper.

2. Dredge chicken in flour, shaking off excess.

3. In a Dutch oven or deep skillet with a cover, heat 1 tablespoon olive oil.

4. Add chicken and brown on all sides. Remove chicken from Dutch oven or skillet.

5. Add remaining tablespoon olive oil to Dutch oven or skillet.

6. Add onion and garlic. Sauté until softened.

7. Stir in chicken broth, tomato paste, and olives, and bring to a boil. Season to taste with salt and pepper.

8. Return chicken to Dutch oven or skillet. Cover and simmer approximately 20 minutes until tender, turning chicken twice during cooking.

grilled chicken three ways

MEAT

Two marinades and one rub offer three new ways to grill chicken at your next barbecue.

herbed honey mustard:

5   garlic cloves, crushed

4   tablespoons olive oil

8   tablespoons Dijon mustard

8   tablespoons honey

4   teaspoons salt

4   teaspoons chopped fresh rosemary
     (may substitute fresh thyme)

½   teaspoon pepper

6   boneless skinless chicken breasts

1. Combine first 7 ingredients together.

2. Add chicken breasts and marinate overnight. Remove chicken from marinade (discard marinade) and grill 8 minutes on each side, or until juices run clear and chicken is no longer pink inside.

tandoori-style rub:

6   tablespoons paprika

2   tablespoons ground coriander

2   tablespoons cumin

2   tablespoons salt

1   tablespoon black pepper

1   tablespoon sugar

1   tablespoon ground ginger

1   teaspoon cinnamon

½   teaspoon cayenne pepper

6   boneless skinless chicken breasts
     (or boneless skinless chicken thighs)

1. Combine first 9 ingredients.

2. Coat chicken breasts in rub and grill 8 minutes on each side, or until juices run clear and chicken is no longer pink inside.

hot *and* spicy marinade:

⅔ cup oil

2 tablespoons pepper

1 tablespoon garlic powder

1 teaspoon red pepper flakes

1 tablespoon lemon juice

½ cup dry red wine

½ cup red wine vinegar

4 tablespoons soy sauce

3 garlic cloves, crushed

2-3 drops hot sauce (optional)

8 boneless skinless chicken breasts
   (or boneless skinless chicken thighs)

1. Combine first 10 ingredients and transfer to zip-top bag.

2. Add chicken and marinate overnight. Remove chicken from marinade (discard marinade) and grill 8 minutes on each side, or until juices run clear and chicken is no longer pink inside.

persian duck *in* pomegranate sauce

A gorgeous restaurant-quality dish that would be ideal for a holiday or romantic anniversary dinner.

1   duck, quartered

2   onions, chopped

1   tablespoon chopped garlic

2   Bosc pears, chopped into 1-inch pieces

2   cups unsweetened pomegranate juice

¼   cup pomegranate syrup

1¼ cups chicken broth

1   tablespoon lemon juice

½   cup chopped dried apricots

1. Preheat oven to 375 degrees.

2. Score duck skin by making several small slits through the skin without cutting into the duck. Place duck, skin side down, in skillet over medium heat. Sear duck and render fat, approximately 5 minutes. Drain fat and reserve for preparing sauce.

3. Transfer duck pieces to a baking dish, placing skin side up, and bake in preheated oven for 1 hour.

4. While duck is cooking, prepare sauce. Heat approximately 2 tablespoons reserved duck fat in the same pan used to sear ducks. Sauté onions until softened. Add garlic and pears; sauté for 5-10 minutes. Add pomegranate juice, pomegranate syrup, and chicken broth. Simmer for about 20 minutes. Sauce should thicken.

5. Stir in lemon juice and dried apricots and remove from heat.

6. When duck has baked for 1 hour, pour sauce on top and bake uncovered for an additional 20 minutes.

Notes: There are many brands of pomegranate syrup (sometimes called pomegranate molasses or pomegranate sauce), with varying degrees of sweetness. Taste sauce after cooking it, before you pour it over duck or chicken. If it is too sweet, add lemon juice to taste. If too tart, add more apricots or some brown sugar and cook an additional 5 minutes.

There is a Sephardic dish called Fesenjan that is very similar to the above recipe, but it is cooked with chopped or ground nuts in sauce. You may add 1½ cups finely chopped walnuts, pecans, almonds, or filberts to sauce. Sauce will be thicker with a consistency similar to chili.

turkey burgers

MEAT

Even a loyal beef eater won't be able to resist these burgers.

¼   cup Worcestershire sauce

¼   cup ketchup

2   tablespoons soy sauce

2   garlic cloves, minced and mashed to a paste
       with ½ teaspoon salt

1   teaspoon chili powder

¼   teaspoon ground cumin

¼   teaspoon Tabasco™ sauce

      Salt and pepper, to taste

2   pounds ground turkey

1   small onion, minced

½   cup fresh breadcrumbs

      Buns or pita bread

1. In a small bowl, stir together Worcestershire sauce, ketchup, soy sauce, garlic paste, chili powder, cumin, Tabasco sauce, salt, and pepper until sauce is smooth. Sauce may be made several days in advance. Store refrigerated.

2. In a separate bowl, mix turkey, onion, breadcrumbs, and ¼ cup of the sauce from Step 1, until well combined. Form into 6 ¾-inch-thick patties.

Note: *Burgers may be prepared up to this point 1 day ahead and chilled, covered.*

3. Divide remaining sauce in half. Half will be used for brushing burgers on the grill and half for drizzling on cooked burgers.

4. Prepare grill. Set oiled rack 5-6 inches over glowing coals. Place burgers on the rack, brushing frequently with sauce from 1 bowl of the sauce, and grill approximately 6 minutes on each side, or until cooked through. Alternately, turkey burgers may be broiled. Use care not to overcook or burgers will be dry.

5. Drizzle burgers with remaining sauce and serve with buns or pita.

herbed cornish game hens

These hens are an upscale, elegant alternative to the standard roast chicken. Depending on size serve either a whole or half hen per person.

4-5 pounds Cornish game hens (3-4 hens)

4 tablespoons olive oil, divided

Salt and pepper, to taste

1 lemon, quartered

4 sprigs fresh rosemary, divided

24 cloves garlic

⅓ cup white wine

⅓ cup low-sodium chicken broth

1. Preheat oven to 450 degrees.

2. Rub hens with 2 tablespoons of the olive oil. Lightly season hens with salt and pepper.

3. Place 1 lemon wedge and 1 sprig rosemary in cavity of each hen. Arrange in a large, heavy roasting pan, and arrange garlic cloves around hens.

4. Roast in preheated oven for 25 minutes.

5. Reduce oven temperature to 350 degrees.

6. In a mixing bowl, whisk together wine, chicken broth, and remaining 2 tablespoons of the oil; pour over hens. Continue roasting about 25 minutes longer, basting with pan juices every 10 minutes, until hens are golden brown and juices run clear.

7. Transfer hens to a platter, pouring any cavity juices into the roasting pan. Remove lemons from cavities and discard. Cover hens with aluminum foil to keep warm.

8. Transfer pan juices and garlic cloves to a medium saucepan and boil about 6 minutes until liquids reduce to a sauce consistency.

9. Serve hens whole or cut hens in half lengthwise and arrange on plates.

10. Spoon sauce and garlic around hens. Garnish with remainder of rosemary sprigs, and serve.

chicken *and* sausage cacciatore

An adaptable dish that will work beautifully served over your favorite pasta or grain.

3   tablespoons extra-virgin olive oil, divided

4   large chicken thighs with skin and bones
     (about 1⅓ pounds)

     Salt and pepper, to taste

¾   pound mild or hot chicken or turkey sausages
     cut on diagonal into 2-inch pieces

¾   pound large mushrooms, quartered

2   pints grape tomatoes

½   cup dry red wine

3   large garlic cloves, pressed

1½   teaspoons chopped fresh rosemary

½   cup coarsely chopped fresh basil

1   can (28 ounce) crushed tomatoes

1. Heat 2 tablespoons of the oil in large nonstick skillet over medium-high heat.

2. Sprinkle chicken with salt and pepper. Add chicken and sausages to skillet. Sauté until brown, 4-5 minutes per side.

3. Transfer chicken and sausages to bowl.

4. Add mushrooms to skillet. Sauté about 4 minutes until brown.

5. Remove from skillet and add to bowl with chicken and sausages.

6. Add remaining 1 tablespoon oil to skillet. Add tomatoes, red wine, garlic, rosemary, and crushed tomatoes. Cover, reduce heat to medium, and cook about 5 minutes until fresh tomatoes soften.

7. Using a potato masher, lightly crush half of the tomatoes.

8. Reduce heat to medium-low. Simmer uncovered 5 minutes.

9. Return chicken, sausages, and mushrooms to skillet and simmer uncovered, turning often, about 15 minutes until chicken and sausages are cooked through.

10. Remove chicken and sausages from skillet and place on platter.

11. Stir basil into sauce in skillet. Season sauce to taste with salt and pepper.

12. Spoon sauce over chicken.

curried chicken salad

Sweet and savory, crunchy and chewy — this salad has something for everyone.

dressing:

3   tablespoons light olive oil

3   tablespoons curry powder

1½ cups mayonnaise

salad:

3   cups cubed cooked chicken

1   cup chopped celery

¼   cup chopped red onion

¼   cup raisins

⅓   cup cashews

1. Combine olive oil and curry powder in a small sauté pan and stir over low heat until fragrant, approximately 30-60 seconds. Combine well with mayonnaise.

2. Combine chicken and dressing, tossing until well coated.

3. Add celery, red onion, and raisins.

4. Refrigerate. Add cashews prior to serving.

white bean *and* turkey chili

MEAT

Hearty and filling. A quick and easy dinner that provides comfort in the cold winter months.

1   tablespoon olive oil

1   pound ground turkey (93% lean)

½   teaspoon salt

1   medium onion, chopped

1   tablespoon smoked paprika

2   teaspoons chili powder

1   tablespoon ground cumin

1   can (28 ounce) crushed tomatoes

1   can (15-19 ounce) white kidney beans
     (cannellini), rinsed and drained

½   cup water

1   green onion (scallion), chopped

½   cup crushed tortilla chips

1. Heat oil in a 12-inch skillet over medium-high heat. Add turkey and salt; cook 6-8 minutes, or until turkey loses its pink color throughout, stirring with the side of a spoon to break it up.

2. Add onion and cook 4 minutes.

3. Stir in smoked paprika, chili powder, and cumin; cook 1 minute.

4. Add crushed tomatoes, beans, and water; heat on high to boiling.

5. Reduce heat to medium and cook uncovered 10 minutes, stirring occasionally.

6. Ladle chili into serving bowls and top with green onions and tortilla chips.

chicken pot pie

A warming one-pot meal to use up leftover chicken or turkey.

4   tablespoons oil

1   onion, chopped

2   cloves garlic, chopped

2   carrots, cleaned and chopped

1   cup corn

1   cup green beans, cut into 1-inch pieces

½   cup sliced zucchini or yellow squash (optional)

½   cup shelled edamame or lima beans (optional)

1   cup sliced mushrooms (optional)

2-3 cups cooked chicken or turkey, cut into large chunks

4   tablespoons flour

2   cups chicken stock

1   tablespoon tomato paste

1   tablespoon tamari

1   teaspoon dried thyme

    Salt and pepper, to taste

1   biscuit dough recipe (page 117), 1 pie crust or sheet puff pastry, thawed

1. Preheat oven to 375 degrees.

2. To assemble the pot pie filling, heat oil in a large ovenproof skillet or Dutch oven.

3. Sauté onions and garlic until onions begin to soften.

4. Add carrots and other vegetables, including optional mushrooms, squash, edamame, or lima beans. Continue to cook, stirring often, until vegetables begin to soften. Add chicken and stir to combine.

5. Sprinkle flour evenly over vegetables and chicken. Gently mix until everything is coated with flour.

6. Stir in chicken stock, mixing well. Simmer gently, uncovered, for 5 minutes until sauce begins to thicken.

7. Stir in tomato paste and tamari. Season the stew with thyme, salt and pepper and remove from heat.

8. Lightly flour a board and roll biscuit dough, pie crust, or puff pastry sheet into a circle large enough to cover the filling. Place dough on top of pot pie filling. Cut several slits in dough.

9. Place pot pie in preheated oven and bake for 30-45 minutes until biscuit topping is browned and pot pie is bubbling.

meat

not your mother's meatloaf

This makes a big batch, which can be cut into individual servings and frozen for quick easy dinners.

½ pound carrots, cleaned and chunked

1 large sweet onion, quartered

3 cloves garlic, minced

2 tablespoons olive oil

   Salt and pepper, to taste

1 box frozen spinach, thawed and squeezed dry

2 pounds lean ground beef

1 cup (or more) fresh breadcrumbs

1 egg, beaten

1 teaspoon paprika

3-5 tablespoons ketchup

3 tablespoons chili sauce

1-3 tablespoons rice or soy milk to moisten, more if needed

1. Preheat oven to 425 degrees.

2. Grind carrots and onion in food processor until very finely chopped. Add in garlic and pulse. Heat olive oil in pan and sauté vegetables 5-10 minutes, until tender. Season to taste with salt and pepper.

3. Transfer to large bowl.

4. Sauté spinach in same pan, then place in bowl with other vegetables.

5. When cool, add in remainder of ingredients and mix well to combine.

6. Grease a large jelly-roll pan.

7. Form meatloaf mixture into 2 large loaf shapes with space in between the 2 loaves. You can also prepare this recipe in small loaf pans.

8. Bake in preheated oven for 1-1¼ hours. Meatloaf is done when meat thermometer registers 140-160°F. When cooked, remove from oven and let rest before slicing. Terrific served cold.

three kinds of sliders

With a choice of Asian, Mediterranean, and Spicy flavoring, this dish will satisfy every slider craving.

1-2 pounds ground beef, bison, veal, turkey, or chicken (or mixture)

Grape tomatoes, sliced thin

1   small onion, sliced thin

Small rolls-ciabiatta, potato, soft, or biscuits

Note: For this recipe, we estimate that one pound of meat will yield 8 sliders.

asian:

2   tablespoons tamari, shoyu, or soy sauce

1   tablespoon grated ginger

1   tablespoon minced or mashed garlic

2   teaspoons honey or brown sugar

3   scallions, finely sliced, including green parts

1   tablespoon sesame oil

1-2 teaspoons potato starch, arrowroot, or cornstarch

1   tablespoon chopped parsley

1   tablespoon chopped cilantro

½   teaspoon finely chopped fresh chili (optional)

¼   teaspoon salt

1   teaspoon pepper

Note: This recipe is for 1 pound ground beef or bison.

mediterranean:

1   tablespoon capers

2   tablespoons minced parsley

1   tablespoon minced cilantro

1   tablespoon chopped or minced garlic

1-2 tablespoons olive oil

1-2 tablespoons chopped basil or a mixture of basil, thyme, and oregano

1   small onion, minced

1-2 teaspoons smoked paprika

1   teaspoon grated lemon rind (optional)

½   teaspoon salt

Fresh ground pepper

Note: This recipe is for 1 pound ground beef, bison, or veal; ground chicken or turkey works well, too.

spicy:

1-2 teaspoons minced chipotle in adobo sauce

1   tablespoon oil

1   small onion, minced

1-2 tablespoons finely chopped parsley (optional)

1   tablespoon minced garlic

1   teaspoon brown sugar or honey

½   teaspoon salt, to taste

¼   teaspoon liquid smoke (optional)

Note: This recipe is for 1 pound ground beef, bison, or turkey.

1. Gently mix meat with choice of flavorings. Avoid overmixing by using hands to combine ingredients into meat. Moisten hands with water and gently form meat into small patties, approximately ½-¾-inch-thick and 1½-2-inches across.

2. Place on a lightly oiled tray.

3. Spray or brush with oil.

4. Sliders may be refrigerated covered for several hours before cooking.

5. Grill or broil until rare or medium-rare.

6. Serve on rolls topped with tomatoes and onion.

barbecue pulled beef sandwiches

Smoky beef cooked until mouth-wateringly tender.

2-3 tablespoons oil

4 pounds chuck roast, brisket, or boneless short ribs (meat should be fatty)

Salt and pepper, to taste

1 lemon, halved

1 large onion, sliced into half moons

4-6 cloves garlic, coarsely chopped

6 tablespoons vinegar, cider or rice

¼ cup brown sugar

3 tablespoons Worcestershire sauce

1 cup ketchup

3 tablespoons tamari or soy sauce

1 bottle or can beer or 1½ cups dry red wine

1 tablespoon liquid smoke (optional)

1-2 teaspoons hot sauce, to taste (optional)

5 cups water or beef broth

1. Preheat oven to 350 degrees.

2. Heat oil in a large Dutch oven. Brown beef on all sides; season to taste with salt and pepper. Remove beef and set aside.

3. Add onion and garlic to pot. Stir and cook until onion begins to soften.

4. Reduce heat and add remaining ingredients (including lemon rind) except meat. Stir well, scraping bottom of pot to loosen crispy bits and combine.

5. Add meat to pot. If necessary, add additional water or stock to just cover meat.

6. Cover Dutch oven and bring to a simmer.

7. Place covered pot in preheated oven for 3-4 hours until meat is tender and falling apart. (Alternately, meat can be braised on the stove for about 4 hours, turning every 2 hours until falling apart.)

8. When meat is ready, remove pot from oven. Transfer meat from pot to a platter until cool enough to shred. Reserve sauce.

9. Remove lemon from sauce and discard.

10. Meanwhile, simmer sauce uncovered until thickened, 15-25 minutes.

11. Shred beef and add back to simmering sauce along with any collected juices. Continue cooking, if necessary, until meat is coated.

12. Adjust seasoning with salt, pepper, and hot sauce.

13. Serve on soft buns with tangy coleslaw.

out-of-this-world veal meatballs *with* mushroom sauce

The depth of flavor in these meatballs is out of this world. A no-brainer for your next holiday meal.

meatballs:

4	teaspoons margarine or olive oil
2	eggs
1	onion
1½	teaspoons salt
	Pepper to taste
2	slices white bread
1	pound chopped veal
1	pound ground beef
2	teaspoons matzo meal
	Flour for dredging
4	tablespoons oil

sauce:

10-12	ounces sliced mushrooms (a mixture of shiitake, cremini, and button mushrooms)
1	cup water
1⅓	cups beef broth
1⅓	cups dry red wine

1. Combine margarine or oil, eggs, onion, salt, pepper, and bread in food processor and blend until a smooth paste is formed.

2. Mix paste into veal and ground beef. Add matzo meal. Let stand for 30 minutes at room temperature or refrigerated for several hours or overnight.

3. Roll into balls and dredge in flour. Heat oil in a skillet and brown meatballs. Remove and place in a separate pan; set aside. Reserve drippings.

4. To prepare sauce, brown mushrooms in drippings. Add water with beef stock and red wine to mushrooms. Simmer sauce until slightly thickened, about 10 minutes.

5. Add meatballs to sauce and cook on medium heat for 30 minutes.

Note: If freezing, don't cook for the last half-hour. The meatballs will cook when reheated.

braised short ribs *with* red wine

A rich, melt-in-your-mouth dish.

1 bottle red wine

1 tablespoon olive oil

3 pounds beef short ribs, cut 2 inches thick

6 medium carrots, cut into ¼-inch slices

3 stalks celery, trimmed and chopped into small slices

4 onions, coarsely chopped

1 head garlic, halved crosswise

7 sprigs thyme

1 bay leaf

½ cup beef broth

½ cup light brown sugar

3 tablespoons tomato paste

½ cup all-purpose flour

1. Preheat oven to 300 degrees.

2. In a large saucepan, boil wine until reduced by about half. Remove from heat and set aside.

3. Meanwhile, place a large, wide Dutch oven over high heat. Add olive oil and when it is very hot, add short ribs and sear until well browned on all sides. Transfer short ribs to a platter.

4. Return Dutch oven to medium-high heat. Add carrots, celery, onions, garlic, thyme, and bay leaf. Sauté about 3 minutes until lightly browned.

5. Add broth and continue to sauté until vegetables are tender, another 1-2 minutes, scraping up any browned bits on the bottom of the pan.

6. Add brown sugar and tomato paste. Cook, stirring, another 2-3 minutes.

7. Return short ribs to Dutch oven and sprinkle with flour. Cook, stirring well until flour is incorporated and beginning to brown.

8. Add reduced wine and bring to a boil. Skim any foam. Cover, leaving lid slightly ajar, and transfer to oven. Cook about 3 hours until meat is very tender and falling off the bone. Short ribs may be served on the bone or meat removed and served in chunks or shreds.

9. To serve sauce, strain vegetables and any liquid from Dutch oven, pressing down to extract as much liquid as possible; discard bay leaf and solids.

10. To remove fat from sauce, skim surface or chill and then skim excess fat, reheat, and serve over or mixed with short ribs.

persian lamb stew

Date syrup, red wine, and beef stock combine for a rich, unforgettable flavor.

4-5 onions, chopped

2　tablespoons olive oil

4　lamb shanks

6-8 carrots, peeled and quartered

1　cup date syrup

1　cup dry red wine

1　cup beef stock or water

1. Preheat oven to 325 degrees.

2. In a skillet sauté onions in olive oil until caramelized; remove to large baking pan. In the same skillet brown lamb shanks by cooking on high heat for 2-3 minutes on each side.

3. Arrange lamb shanks and carrots with onions in the baking pan.

4. In a small bowl, combine date syrup, red wine, and stock (or water), then pour over lamb in baking pan. Cover and cook in preheated oven for 2-3 hours.

5. Remove lamb shanks from pan, remove meat from bone, discard bone, and replace lamb meat in the stew until served.

6. Serve alone or over Persian rice or couscous.

london broil *with* chimichurri

Chimichurri, the classic Argentinean condiment, makes a star out of the London broil in this dish.

london broil:

Shoulder London broil
  (approximately 1½-2 pounds)

3   cloves garlic, minced or pressed

½   cup extra-virgin olive oil

Salt and pepper, to taste

chimichurri:

1   clove garlic, peeled

⅓   cup chopped parsley

3   tablespoons extra-virgin olive oil

1   tablespoon lemon juice

1   tablespoon red wine vinegar

¾   teaspoon dried oregano

½   teaspoon hot red pepper flakes

Salt and pepper, to taste

1. Marinate London broil in garlic, olive oil, salt, and pepper for 1 hour at room temperature.

2. Remove meat from marinade. Grill to medium-rare. Let rest for 10 minutes.

3. To prepare chimichurri, chop garlic in food processor. Add parsley and chop further. Transfer mixture to a bowl. Add remaining ingredients and stir to combine.

4. Slice London broil against grain in thick slices and serve with chimichurri.

rib-eye steak *with* tomato-caper relish

A fresh take on flavoring for rib-eye. This relish is versatile enough to be used on grilled chicken or burgers.

steaks:

2   rib-eye steaks (approximately 1 pound each)

3   teaspoons ground cumin

Salt and freshly ground pepper, to taste

tomato-caper relish:

Kosher salt

1   clove garlic, chopped

2   red and 2 yellow tomatoes, cut into cubes

3   tablespoons chopped pimento-stuffed olives

5   tablespoons chopped fresh cilantro

3   tablespoons extra-virgin olive oil, divided

2   tablespoons capers, drained

1½ tablespoons fresh lime juice

1   fresh jalapeño pepper, minced

½   teaspoon dried oregano

Salt and pepper, to taste

1. Sprinkle steaks with cumin, salt, and pepper.

2. Grill steaks or sear in skillet to medium-rare (approximately 6-7 minutes per side).

3. Remove from grill or skillet. Let steaks rest 10 minutes.

4. To prepare relish, sprinkle salt on garlic and mash to a paste. Transfer garlic to a bowl.

5. Add tomatoes, olives, cilantro, olive oil, capers, lime juice, jalapeño, and oregano. Toss to blend. Season to taste with salt and pepper.

6. Slice steak and serve with the relish.

Note: Tomato-caper relish can be made 1-3 hours in advance and left at room temperature.

beer-basted pot roast

The perfect dish for the "meat and potatoes" lover in your life.

5	tablespoons olive oil
5	pounds pot roast (chuck eye roast)
1	cup chopped onion
2	pounds mushrooms, sliced
2	bottles beer plus the equivalent of 1 bottle of water
¼	teaspoon seasoned salt or to taste
⅛	teaspoon pepper
½	teaspoon thyme
10-12	small red bliss potatoes

1. Preheat oven to 350 degrees.

2. Heat oil in a large skillet over medium heat. Brown meat on all sides.

3. Transfer roast to a Dutch oven.

4. Pour off excess grease from skillet, leaving about 1 tablespoon.

5. Add onion and mushrooms; sauté until onion is tender.

6. Add beer, water, salt, pepper, and thyme. Bring mixture to a boil; pour over roast.

7. Cover and bake in preheated oven for 2 hours.

8. Add potatoes to pan, cover, and continue roasting for an additional 1 hour until meat and potatoes are tender.

traditional rib roast

A prime cut of meat like a rib roast requires only the simplest ingredients and preparation to bring out its natural goodness.

1   (5-rib) prime rib beef roast, about 8 pounds

5   cloves garlic, crushed

2   tablespoons roughly chopped fresh rosemary
     and thyme

1   teaspoon salt

2   teaspoons freshly cracked pepper

3-4 tablespoons olive oil

1. Preheat oven to 325 degrees.

2. Place roast, rib side down, in a large roasting pan.

3. In a small bowl mash together garlic, rosemary, thyme, salt, pepper, and olive oil to make a paste. Smear paste generously over the entire roast. Roast for about 2½ hours, or approximately 20 minutes per pound for medium-rare.

4. Check the internal temperature of roast in several places with an instant-read meat thermometer. It should register 120-125 degrees for medium-rare.

5. Remove beef to a carving board and allow to rest for 20 minutes to let the juices settle before slicing.

Note: The internal temperature of the meat will continue to rise about 10 degrees once removed from the oven.

veal marsala

Reducing the sauce makes for a supremely satisfying, distinctive flavor.

3 pounds veal medallions or boneless cutlets (¼-inch thick)

½ cup flour

Salt and pepper, to taste

6 tablespoons olive oil, divided

3 large shallots, minced

2 pounds fresh mushrooms, sliced

1 cup Marsala wine

3 cloves garlic, minced

1½ cups beef stock

1. Preheat oven to 250 degrees.

2. Lightly coat veal medallions in flour, and season to taste with salt and pepper.

3. Heat 1 tablespoon of the olive oil in a skillet over medium-high heat.

4. Cook veal in the heated skillet about 5 minutes, just until cooked through.

5. Remove from the skillet, place in a baking dish covered with foil, and keep warm in the preheated oven until ready to serve.

6. Heat remaining olive oil in the skillet over medium-low heat.

7. Sauté shallots and mushrooms, scraping up any browned bits until shallots are tender. Increase heat to medium-high, and stir in Marsala and garlic. Cook and stir until thickened.

8. Add beef stock to the skillet. Continue to cook, stirring frequently until sauce is reduced by half, about 1 cup.

9. To serve, spoon sauce with mushrooms over veal.

mediterranean brisket

A mixture of savory and sweet ingredients brings out the flavor of the meat. For the busy cook, this dish can be made up to 2 days ahead and then reheated.

⅔ cup golden raisins, divided

10-12 dried apricots

9 large cloves garlic, divided

3½ teaspoons ground cumin, divided

1 teaspoon salt

¼ teaspoon ground cinnamon

¼ teaspoon ground black pepper

4½-5 pounds beef brisket

3 tablespoons olive oil

4 cups chopped onion

2 medium carrots, coarsely chopped

1 tablespoon minced fresh ginger

⅛ teaspoon cayenne pepper

1 cup dry red wine

3 cups beef stock

⅔ cup pitted prunes, quartered

1. Combine ⅓ cup of raisins, apricots, 3 garlic cloves, 1 teaspoon cumin, salt, cinnamon, and pepper in food processor. Pulse chop to coarse purée; reserve 1 tablespoon of this mixture for later use.

2. Using a small sharp knife, make ½-inch-deep slits all over brisket. Press apricot mixture into slits.

3. Position rack in bottom third of oven and preheat to 300 degrees.

4. Heat oil in heavy large ovenproof pot over medium-high heat. Sprinkle brisket all over with salt and pepper. Add brisket to pot and sauté about 5 minutes per side until brown.

5. Transfer to plate, fat side up. Spread with reserved apricot mixture.

6. Add onions to same pot. Sauté over medium-high heat 5 minutes.

7. Add carrots, ginger, cayenne pepper, remaining garlic cloves, and cumin; sauté 3 minutes.

8. Add wine and boil about 5 minutes until reduced almost to glaze, stirring up any browned bits.

9. Return brisket to pot. Add stock and bring to simmer.

10. Spoon some of the vegetable mixture over brisket. Cover pot and place in oven. Roast brisket 3 hours, basting every 30 minutes with pan juices.

11. Add prunes and remaining ⅓ cup raisins. Cover; roast about 30 minutes until brisket is tender.

12. Cool brisket uncovered 1 hour. Chill uncovered until cold, then cover and refrigerate overnight.

13. Skim off any solid fat that rises to the top of the gravy and discard. Scrape gravy off brisket into pot. Place brisket on work surface. Slice brisket thinly against the grain.

14. Bring gravy in pot to boil over medium-high heat. Cook to thicken slightly, if desired. Season gravy to taste with salt and pepper.

15. Arrange sliced brisket in large ovenproof dish. Spoon gravy over brisket. Cover with foil. (Can be made 2 days ahead; refrigerate.)

16. Warm covered brisket in a 350-degree oven about 30 minutes (or 40 minutes if chilled).

stuffed breast of veal

A beautiful holiday dish that is worth the extra effort.

stuffing:

1   small onion, diced

2   tablespoons canola oil

4   Kaiser rolls, torn into 1-inch pieces

5   eggs or 2 eggs and 3 egg whites

   A few sprigs fresh parsley, chopped

   Salt, to taste

veal:

4-5 pounds breast of veal trimmed of excess fat
    with a deep pocket for the stuffing

½   large onion, sliced

2-3 cloves garlic, thinly sliced

1   teaspoon minced garlic

3   tablespoons oil

1   teaspoon paprika

½   cup sweet wine

2   tablespoons ketchup

1. To prepare stuffing, heat oil in frying pan and sauté onion.

2. Moisten rolls with water. Squeeze excess water out and place in pan with sautéed onion.

3. Beat eggs in a bowl with a fork. Add parsley to eggs. Mix in a pinch of salt. Pour egg mixture into the pan. Cook gently until eggs are set. Remove pan from heat.

4. Place cooled stuffing into the pocket of the veal. Set aside leftover stuffing to roast alongside the veal.

5. Preheat oven to 400 degrees.

6. Line the bottom of a large roasting pan with sliced onions. Place stuffed veal on top of onions. Using a sharp knife, make shallow slits in the veal.

7. Insert garlic slices into slits. Mix minced garlic and paprika with oil. Spread over meat. Mix ketchup and wine until smooth. Pour over meat. Place remaining stuffing beside the meat in the pan.

8. Pour about 1½ cups of water into the bottom of the pan. Cover roast tightly with foil.

9. Roast in preheated oven for at least 2-2½ hours. Baste meat with juices every 30 minutes. Add additional water, if necessary.

10. Continue roasting until veal is soft when pierced with a paring knife. Remove from oven. Let roast rest 10 minutes. If desired, meat can be cooled and stored overnight in the refrigerator.

11. Slice and serve with gravy. If refrigerated, slice and reheat with gravy at 350 degrees until warmed through.

rosemary grilled lamb chops

Marinate these lamb chops overnight to let the flavors sink in.

10-12 loin shoulder chops, about ½-inch thick

½   cup olive oil

⅓   cup red wine vinegar

1   tablespoon fresh rosemary

2   cloves garlic, minced

½   teaspoon salt

¼   teaspoon black pepper

1. Combine all ingredients, except lamb, in a large glass bowl.

2. Place chops in bowl and turn repeatedly to coat well. Cover and refrigerate for 4 hours to overnight.

3. Once marinated, remove chops from refrigerator and allow to come to room temperature.

4. Preheat grill to medium-high heat.

5. Remove chops from marinade and place on a lightly oiled grill rack. Cook for 8 minutes on each side. Remove from heat; allow to rest for 3-5 minutes.

6. Alternately, chops may be broiled.

silver tip roast

Five ingredients & a simple preparation = a perfect Friday night dinner.

4   pounds silver tip (shoulder roast can be substituted)

2   tablespoons horseradish or Dijon mustard

4   cloves garlic, chopped

1   tablespoon cracked black pepper

½   cup dry red wine

1. Preheat oven to 475 degrees.

2. Place meat on roasting rack. Spread the top with horseradish or mustard, garlic, and pepper.

3. Cook in preheated oven for 15 minutes.

4. Turn the heat down to 375 degrees and roast for 15 minutes per pound for rare or 20 minutes per pound for medium.

5. Remove roast from oven. Cover loosely with foil and allow roast to rest for 10 minutes before slicing.

6. Deglaze the roasting pan with red wine. Reduce and pour over sliced meat.

marinated rack of veal

Veal can be Frenched by your butcher upon request.

veal:

Zest of 2 lemons

3   cloves garlic

1   tablespoon fennel seed

1   small bunch basil leaves

1   teaspoon ground white pepper

4   tablespoons extra-virgin olive oil

Rack of veal, Frenched, about 4½ pounds

Salt, to taste

green sauce:

1   bunch fresh flat-leaf parsley

1   bunch fresh mint

1   bunch fresh basil

6   cloves garlic

½   cup red wine vinegar

3   tablespoons sugar

1½ cups extra-virgin olive oil

Salt and white pepper, to taste

1. To prepare veal, place lemon zest, garlic, fennel seed, basil leaves, white pepper, and extra-virgin olive oil into the bowl of a food processor. Purée until all of the ingredients have formed a paste.

2. Place veal in large pan, and rub rack of veal with the paste. Cover and place in the refrigerator for about 6 hours or overnight.

3. Preheat oven to 375 degrees.

4. Remove veal from pan, and discard marinade. Season veal with salt to taste.

5. Place roasting pan over medium-high heat (may cover 2 burners) and add enough oil to coat bottom of pan. Sear veal on all sides, making sure each side has a rich brown sear.

6. Place veal in preheated oven and roast to an internal temperature of 130 degrees for medium-rare, about 1½ hours, or 20 minutes per pound.

7. Remove from oven, and allow roast to rest for at least 15 minutes.

8. To prepare green sauce, add to food processor parsley, mint, basil, garlic, vinegar, sugar, and olive oil, and season to taste with salt and pepper. Pulse until well combined. Serve with veal.

stuffed crown roast of lamb

This is a beauty of a dish, and the taste more than matches its looks.

1   (4-5 pound) crown roast of lamb

2   cloves garlic, slivered

2   tablespoons fresh lemon juice

2   tablespoons coarse salt, divided

½   teaspoon freshly ground pepper

1   small eggplant (about 1 pound), peeled and
      cut into 1-inch cubes

3   tablespoons olive oil, divided

½   cup minced onion

1   celery stalk, minced

1   pound lean ground lamb

1½ cups cooked orzo

½   cup pine nuts or slivered almonds, toasted

¼   cup raisins

¼   cup minced fresh flat-leaf parsley

8   large ripe olives, pitted and chopped

1   teaspoon grated lemon zest

¼   teaspoon ground cardamom

¼   teaspoon ground cinnamon

   Salt and freshly ground pepper, to taste

1. Using a sharp knife make lengthwise slits through roast in several places. Insert a sliver of garlic into each slit. Brush roast with lemon juice, and rub with 1 tablespoon of the salt and pepper.

2. Place roast, bone ends up, in a shallow roasting pan lined with heavy-duty aluminum foil. Set aside.

3. Place cubed eggplant in a large bowl and sprinkle with remaining 1 tablespoon salt; let stand for 15 minutes. Rinse eggplant, and pat dry with paper towel.

4. Preheat oven to 350 degrees.

5. Sauté eggplant in 2 tablespoons oil in a large skillet over medium-high heat, stirring frequently, until tender. Remove eggplant from skillet; set aside.

6. In the same skillet, sauté onion and celery in remaining 1 tablespoon oil over medium-high heat, until tender.

7. Add ground lamb and cook until meat is crumbled and nicely browned; drain.

8. Add reserved eggplant, orzo, pine nuts or almonds, raisins, parsley, chopped olives, lemon rind, cardamom, and cinnamon to meat mixture. Season to taste with salt and pepper.

9. Spoon mixture into center of roast. Cover stuffing and exposed ends of ribs with aluminum foil.

10. Roast in preheated oven for 1 hour and 15 minutes. Remove foil from stuffing and bake an additional 15 minutes or until meat thermometer registers 160 degrees. Remove foil and transfer to a large serving platter. Let stand 10 minutes before slicing and serving.

veal pâté en croûte

A fancier dish for a special occasion. Serve with cornichons as a first course or as a light luncheon dish accompanied by a green salad.

½ cup cognac or dry sherry

3 tablespoons oil

1 cup minced onion

1½ pounds ground veal

1 pound ground beef

6 ounces smoked sausage, chopped into ½-inch pieces

3 garlic cloves, minced

2½ teaspoons salt

2½ teaspoons dried thyme

1½ teaspoons allspice

½ cup shelled pistachios (optional)

1 teaspoon freshly ground black pepper

1 large egg, lightly beaten

¼ cup dairy-free sour cream

2 sheets puff pastry, thawed

1 egg plus 1 tablespoon water, beaten for glaze

1. Preheat oven to 350 degrees.

2. Place cognac in a small pot and bring to a boil over medium-high heat. Boil cognac until reduced to ¼ cup, about 2 minutes. Cool.

3. Heat oil in a heavy medium skillet over medium heat. Add onion and sauté until soft and translucent but not brown, about 8 minutes. Remove from heat and set aside until needed.

4. Combine ground veal, ground beef, and smoked sausage in large bowl, mixing until well blended.

5. Add sautéed onion, garlic, salt, thyme, allspice, pistachios, and pepper to bowl with veal mixture and mix until incorporated.

6. Add egg, sour cream substitute, and reduced cognac. Mix until well blended.

7. Line a large baking sheet with parchment.

8. Unfold a puff pastry sheet and arrange on one half of the prepared sheet. Place half of the veal mixture in the center of pastry sheet, forming into an oblong. Fold sides up to encase veal, pressing edges of pastry together to seal. Turn the packet seam-side down on to the baking sheet. Repeat with second pastry sheet and remaining veal mixture.

9. Cut 3 slits in the top of each pastry packet. If desired, decorate with extra pieces of puff pastry. Brush with egg glaze.

10. Bake in preheated oven until pastry is golden brown, about 1 hour. Pâté is done when an instant read meat thermometer registers 145-150 degrees.

11. Remove from oven and allow pâté to cool. Wrap carefully and refrigerate until cold before slicing and serving.

12. May be stored refrigerated for several days.

vegetarian entrées

vegetarian entrées

chickpea patties

Try these as a healthy alternative to hamburgers!

1	tablespoon extra-virgin olive oil
1	cup finely chopped onion
⅓	cup finely diced carrots
½	cup finely diced celery
¾	cup finely diced sweet red pepper
2	tablespoons chopped flat-leaf parsley
1	teaspoon minced garlic
⅛	teaspoon ground cumin
1½-2	tablespoons soy sauce
1	cup cooked chickpeas
⅛	cup tahini
1	egg
½	cup flour for dredging

1. Preheat oven to 350 degrees.

2. Cover a medium baking pan with parchment paper, and set aside.

3. In a large skillet, heat oil and add onion, carrots, celery, red pepper, and parsley. Sauté for 7-8 minutes.

4. Add garlic, cumin, and soy sauce; mix together and sauté another 30 seconds.

5. Place chickpeas in a food processor with tahini and egg; process until mashed, scraping sides of bowl as needed.

6. In a large bowl, combine sautéed vegetables with chickpea mixture and adjust seasoning.

7. Wet hands slightly and form mixture into 10 patties (approximately 2½ inches in diameter). Dredge both sides in flour.

8. Heat oil in a pan and sauté patties until golden brown.

9. Transfer patties to prepared baking sheet. Bake 12-15 minutes on one side, turn them over, and bake 10-12 minutes on the other side.

10. Serve hot.

leek *and* artichoke frittata

From the Italian verb "to fry," a frittata is a cross between an omelet and a quiche. Try this at your next Sunday brunch or Shavuot lunch.

1   large leek (½ pound), white and light green
    parts only, rinsed well, halved, and sliced

2   tablespoons extra-virgin olive oil, divided

2   cloves garlic, minced

1   box frozen artichokes (5 or 6 ounce), thawed
    and sliced in half

1   teaspoon chopped fresh rosemary leaves

8   large eggs

1½ teaspoons salt, divided

½   cup low-fat ricotta cheese

    Freshly ground black pepper

1. In a 10-inch ovenproof nonstick frying pan over medium heat, cook leek in 1 tablespoon of the olive oil, stirring often, 5-7 minutes until very tender.

2. Stir in garlic; cook, stirring, about 1 minute until fragrant.

3. Add thawed artichokes and rosemary; cook briefly, stirring to coat with oil. Remove from heat. Stir in 1 teaspoon salt.

4. Whisk eggs in a bowl. Beat in remaining ½ teaspoon salt and ricotta cheese. Stir in cooked artichokes and leek. Add pepper to taste.

5. Preheat broiler.

6. Wipe out frying pan and set over medium heat. Add remaining tablespoon oil. When oil is hot, pour in egg mixture; cook 1 minute, stirring occasionally to distribute cheese and greens. Continue cooking, tilting pan and using a spatula to lift up the frittata's outer edge and let eggs run underneath until eggs no longer flow easily.

7. Turn heat to low and cover pan. Cook 6-10 minutes until frittata is almost set.

8. Broil frittata about 3 inches from heating element for about 2 minutes until just beginning to color on top; remove from oven. Let frittata rest in pan about 5 minutes.

9. Loosen edges with a spatula and carefully slide out onto a platter. Cool to warm room temperature and cut into diamonds or wedges.

Note: Frittata can be made up to 1 day before slicing. Store covered in refrigerator. Bring to room temperature to serve.

shakshuka *(eggs poached in tomato sauce)*

This delicious dish originated in North Africa and was brought to Israel by Tunisian Jews.

¼ cup olive oil

1 small yellow onion, chopped

5 cloves garlic, crushed then sliced

1 teaspoon ground cumin

1 tablespoon paprika

1 can (28 ounce) whole peeled tomatoes, undrained

½ cup water

Salt and pepper, to taste

6 eggs

1 tablespoon chopped flat-leaf parsley

Warm pita, for serving

1. Heat oil in a 12-inch skillet over medium-high heat. Add onion and cook, stirring occasionally, about 6 minutes until onion is soft and golden brown.

2. Add garlic, cumin, and paprika; cook, stirring frequently, about 2 minutes until garlic is soft.

3. Place tomatoes and their liquid into a medium bowl and crush with your hands. Add crushed tomatoes and their liquid to skillet along with water and stir together with garlic/spice mixture.

4. Reduce heat to medium and simmer, stirring occasionally, about 15 minutes until tomato mixture thickens slightly.

5. Season sauce to taste with salt and pepper.

6. Carefully crack eggs (so as to not break yolks) over sauce so that eggs are evenly distributed across the sauce's surface. Cover skillet and cook about 5 minutes until yolks are just set. Do not overcook; yolks should be set but a little runny on the inside.

7. Once yolks are just set, delicately baste whites of the eggs with tomato mixture, being careful not to disturb the yolks.

8. Sprinkle shakshuka with parsley.

9. Serve hot from the pan with pita for dipping.

vegetable moussaka

DAIRY

Although traditionally a dish unavailable to the kosher home due to its mix of meat and cheese, you can now enjoy the flavor of moussaka in this elegant vegetarian version.

moussaka:

3½ pounds eggplant, unpeeled, cut into ½-inch-thick rounds

Salt

Olive oil or olive oil spray, for coating eggplant and greasing pan

¼ cup olive oil, for cooking vegetables

1 large onion, thinly sliced

1 cup finely chopped peeled carrots

1 cup finely chopped celery

4 cloves garlic, minced

12 ounces portobello mushrooms, cut into ½-inch pieces

1 teaspoon dried oregano

½ teaspoon ground cinnamon

1 can (28 ounce) crushed tomatoes with juice

¼ cup chopped fresh Italian parsley

1 cup grated Parmesan cheese, divided

Black pepper, to taste

1. Cover 2 baking sheets with paper towels.

2. Sprinkle both sides of eggplant rounds with salt. Arrange eggplant in single layer atop towels. Let stand 30 minutes.

3. Preheat oven to 425 degrees. Position first rack in bottom third of oven and second rack in top third of oven.

4. Remove eggplant and paper towels from baking sheets. Pat eggplant dry. Oil the same baking sheets. Brush each side of eggplant rounds with olive oil or coat with oil spray. Arrange in single layer on baking sheets. Bake 10 minutes. Turn eggplant and continue baking about 15 minutes until tender. Cool.

5. Reduce oven temperature to 350 degrees.

6. To make tomato sauce, heat oil in heavy large skillet over medium-high heat. Add onion, carrots, and celery. Sauté about 12 minutes until onion is very tender. Add garlic and then mushrooms. Sauté about 10 minutes until liquid evaporates. Mix in oregano and cinnamon. Add tomatoes with their juice and parsley. Cook about 10 minutes until mixture is thick. Season to taste with salt and pepper.

7. Lightly oil a 13x9x2-inch glass baking dish. Arrange half of eggplant rounds in single layer in dish. Spoon half of tomato mixture evenly over eggplant. Sprinkle with 2 tablespoons of the Parmesan. Repeat layering with remaining eggplant, tomato mixture, and 2 tablespoons Parmesan. Set aside.

white sauce:

4   large egg yolks

6   tablespoons (¾ stick) butter

7   tablespoons all-purpose flour

3½ cups whole milk or 2% milk

Pinch nutmeg

Salt and pepper

8. To prepare white sauce, whisk yolks in a bowl and set aside. Melt butter in heavy medium saucepan over medium heat. Whisk in flour to make a thick paste. Gradually whisk in milk, stirring constantly. Simmer about 5 minutes, until sauce thickens, stirring constantly. Whisk in ½ cup of the Parmesan. Season to taste with salt and pepper. Gradually whisk yolks into hot milk mixture.

9. Pour sauce over vegetables in dish. Sprinkle remaining ¼ cup Parmesan over sauce.

Note: *You can stop at this point up to one day in advance of baking. Simply cover and refrigerate.*

10. Bake moussaka in preheated oven about 45 minutes until heated through and sauce is golden brown on top (or about 55 minutes for refrigerated moussaka).

11. Cool 15 minutes and serve warm.

mexican lasagna

A delightful variation on Italian lasagna, this dish mingles our favorite tastes of Mexico.

10	medium to large fresh poblano chilies
1	can (15 ounce) black beans, drained
8-10	corn tortillas, cut in half
2-3	tablespoons oil, more if needed

tomato sauce:

1½	cans (14-16 ounce) whole tomatoes including juice
3	large garlic cloves, chopped
¼	cup chopped fresh cilantro
½	teaspoon sugar
½	teaspoon salt or to taste
3	tablespoons olive oil

goat cheese sauce:

1	cup half-and-half
8	ounces soft mild goat cheese
¼	teaspoon salt or to taste

spinach filling:

1	pound baby spinach
2	tablespoons olive oil
½	teaspoon salt or to taste

1. To prepare chilies, broil 2 inches from heat 8-10 minutes; turn until skins are blackened. Transfer immediately to a large bowl and cover with plastic wrap. When cool enough to handle, peel chilies, then open flat and discard seeds and stems, wiping with paper towels or dunking in a bowl of water briefly, if necessary, to remove seeds. If chilies taste very spicy, cut out ribs with scissors to make them milder. Cut chilies into 1-inch pieces and set aside.

2. To prepare tomato sauce, purée tomatoes with juice, garlic, cilantro, sugar, and salt in a blender. Heat oil in a 10-inch nonstick skillet over moderate heat until hot but not smoking, then add tomato mixture (be careful of splattering) and simmer, stirring until thickened and reduced to about 1 cup, about 6 minutes.

3. To prepare goat cheese sauce, gently simmer half-and-half in a small heavy saucepan, covered, 10 minutes. Whisk in goat cheese and salt; heat over low heat, whisking until smooth.

4. To prepare spinach filling, blanch spinach in batches in a large pot of boiling salted water 1 minute, transferring with a slotted spoon to a large bowl of cold water to cool. Drain in a colander, pressing on spinach with back of a spoon to remove excess water, and then coarsely chop. Alternately, microwave spinach until wilted, approximately 2 minutes. Heat oil in clean nonstick skillet over moderately high heat until hot but not smoking. Sauté spinach, stirring, 2 minutes. Stir in salt and remove from heat.

assemble the lasagna:

1. Preheat oven to 350 degrees.

2. Heat 2-3 tablespoons oil in cleaned nonstick skillet over moderately high heat until hot but not smoking. Fry tortillas in the hot skillet, 2 halves at a time, turning over once until just crisp, about 1 minute total. Transfer tortillas to a paper towel lined plate to drain.

3. Spread ¼ of the tomato sauce over bottom of an 8x10-inch casserole dish.

4. Arrange half of the tortillas on top of tomato sauce layer, spread tomato sauce and sprinkle evenly with black beans.

5. Arrange poblano pieces flat over black beans to cover. Spread half of spinach filling evenly over chilies and drizzle with ¼ cup of the goat cheese sauce.

6. Repeat with another set of layers.

7. Cover with remaining chilies. Spread tomato sauce over chilies and top with remaining tortillas. Cover tortillas with remaining goat cheese sauce, spreading evenly. The final casserole will have 2 spinach, 3 chilie, and 3 tortilla layers.

8. Bake lasagna, covered with foil, 25-30 minutes until bubbling and heated through. Remove from oven.

9. Preheat broiler. Remove foil and broil about 3 inches from heat for about 2 minutes until top is bubbling and beginning to brown. Serve hot.

sweet corn cakes with roasted red peppers

A fresh summery recipe that is colorful and sweet.

2   cups corn, fresh (2-3 cobs of corn) or frozen

1   scallion, finely chopped

Splash whole milk or soy milk

½   cup flour

2   cloves garlic, crushed, divided

2   teaspoons dried oregano, divided

Salt and pepper, to taste

2   eggs, beaten

3   tablespoons olive oil plus more for sautéing

1   large red pepper, cut in thin strips

1. If using fresh corn, place in a pot of cold water and bring to a boil. Cook for 5 minutes. Drain corn and let cool. Cut kernels off the cob into a bowl. Corn should measure approximately 2 cups. If using frozen corn, thaw, measure and set aside until needed.

2. Add scallion, milk, flour, 1 of the crushed garlic cloves, 1 teaspoon of the oregano, salt, and pepper to bowl of corn.

3. Stir eggs into corn mixture. Add more flour, 1 tablespoon at a time, if mixture is too thin.

4. Heat oil in pan. When pan is hot drop a tablespoon of batter into the pan; turn when cake is set. Brown on both sides and remove to pan lined with paper towel to drain.

5. Alternately, drop batter onto an oiled pan and bake in a preheated 400-degree oven 10 minutes until browned.

6. In a separate pan, sauté peppers in olive oil with the remaining garlic and oregano until beginning to soften.

7. Season to taste with salt and pepper. Cook for 3-5 minutes.

8. Serve corn cakes with sautéed peppers on top.

barbecue tempeh

A surprise crowd pleaser at our tasting, it could easily already become part of a regular weeknight repertoire.

1   onion, chopped

2-3 cloves garlic, chopped

2-3 tablespoons oil

½   cup chopped carrots and/or red peppers

1   package (8 ounce) tempeh, cut into 1-inch
    pieces

¼   cup cashews or other nuts (optional)

1-2 tablespoons chili powder (freshly ground dried
    chilies work well)

1-2 teaspoons cumin

    Salt and pepper, to taste

barbecue sauce:

½   cup ketchup

⅓   cup cider vinegar

1-2 tablespoons tamari or soy sauce

1   tablespoon balsamic vinegar

3-4 tablespoons brown sugar

2   teaspoons Dijon mustard

1   tablespoon minced fresh garlic

½   small onion, minced

    Hot sauce or minced chipotle in adobo sauce,
    to taste (optional)

1   tablespoon molasses (or honey)

1   tablespoon hoisin sauce (optional)

1   tablespoon oil

½   teaspoon liquid smoke (optional)

    Salt and pepper, to taste

½   cup water

1. Sauté onion and garlic with oil until softened and fragrant.

2. Add carrots and peppers; cook until glistening.

3. Add tempeh, cashews, and remaining seasonings, stirring gently to mix. Cook until tempeh begins to brown.

4. To prepare barbecue sauce, mix all ingredients together except water. Add barbecue sauce, together with ½ cup water, to the tempeh mix. Stir to coat vegetables and tempeh.

5. Simmer until sauce has thickened, stirring to prevent sticking.

6. Serve hot with rice or noodles.

vegetarian black bean chili

This could become one of your favorite dinners. Serve it over short grain brown rice with sour cream and chopped jalapeños. It also makes a great lunch the next day.

1	cup finely chopped onion
2-3	cloves garlic, minced
2	tablespoons olive oil
1	tablespoon ground cumin
1	tablespoon coriander
1	can (28 ounce) chopped tomatoes
1	cup best quality salsa
1	cup chopped red peppers
6	cups cooked black beans (16 ounces dried beans)
1	cup fresh or frozen corn kernels
	Salt, to taste

1. Sauté onion and garlic in olive oil until golden.

2. Add cumin and coriander and sauté 1-2 minutes.

3. Add tomatoes, salsa, and peppers; cook on a low-to-medium flame for 15 minutes.

4. Add beans and corn; cook on a low-to-medium flame for another 15 minutes.

5. Adjust seasoning to taste.

6. Serve hot over rice.

earthy vegetarian cholent

PARVE

A full-flavored and healthy alternative to meat cholent.

- ½ cup dried white Northern beans
- ½ cup dried kidney beans
- ½ cup dried baby lima beans
- 2 tablespoons vegetable oil
- 3 large onions, diced
- 3 cloves garlic, chopped
- ½ cup barley
- 3 large potatoes, cut into chunks
- 3-4 portobello mushrooms, cut in chunks
- 2 tablespoons tomato paste
- 1 tablespoon soy sauce or tamari
- 1 tablespoon brown sugar or 2 teaspoons honey
- ⅓ cup ketchup
- 1 tablespoon salt
- ½ teaspoon black pepper
- 1 teaspoon paprika
- 6-8 cups water or vegetable stock

1. Combine beans and remaining ingredients in a crock pot. Add water or vegetable stock to cover.

2. Cook overnight on low. Alternatively, cholent may be assembled in a Dutch oven and baked, covered, at 200 degrees overnight.

green peas and potato curry

An authentic vegetarian Indian recipe with complex yet comforting flavors. Can be served as an entrée or as a side dish with fish.

"green masala" paste:

1 serrano chili, or less to taste

2 cloves garlic

½ inch ginger

2-3 tablespoons cilantro leaves

2 tablespoons water

curry:

2-3 tablespoons oil

1 large onion, chopped

1 large tomato, chopped

2 large potatoes, peeled and cut into 1-inch pieces

½ cup water

¼ teaspoon turmeric

1 pound frozen green peas

¼ cup coconut milk

⅓ cup garam masala*

Salt, to taste

1. To prepare "green masala" paste, combine ingredients and blend in a food processor. Set aside.

2. To prepare curry, heat oil in a pan and sauté onion until light brown.

3. Add "green masala" paste, maintaining low-medium heat. Stir for 1 minute.

4. Add chopped onion, chopped tomato, potatoes, water, and turmeric. Stir occasionally to prevent food from sticking.

5. When potatoes are partially cooked, add frozen peas, coconut milk, and garam masala. Season to taste with salt. Cook until potatoes and peas are cooked through.

6. Serve hot over basmati rice or with naan (an Indian bread) or pita bread.

Note: *This Indian spice mixture is available in many supermarkets under hashgachah; however, you can also prepare your own: blend ¼ stick cinnamon, 2-3 whole cloves, 2-3 cardamom pods, and 3 black peppercorns in a food processor or coffee grinder until the ingredients are fully pulverized into a powder.*

potat

An onion-potato-cheese delight! Great dish for a dairy Passover meal.

1   onion, diced

1   tablespoon oil

3   boiled potatoes, sliced

2½ cups grated mozzarella cheese or other mild white cheese

2-3 tablespoons grated Parmesan cheese

3   eggs

1   teaspoon salt

½   teaspoon pepper

½   teaspoon parsley

½   teaspoon garlic

1. Preheat oven to 350 degrees.

2. Grease a 9-inch pie pan.

3. Sauté onion in oil until golden brown. Set aside until needed.

4. Line the bottom of the pan with potato slices.

5. In a bowl, mix mozzarella or white cheese, Parmesan cheese, eggs, and spices. Pour the mixture into the pan on top of the potatoes. Sprinkle with fried onions.

6. Bake in preheated oven for 20 minutes or until egg is set and cooked through.

smoky swiss chard pie

PARVE

Make this pie ahead and reheat for a perfect Shabbat lunch appetizer or substitute for traditional kugel.

⅓   cup olive oil, divided

1   onion, chopped

3-4   cloves garlic, minced

1   pound Swiss chard, cleaned and chopped (or 1 pound mixed greens, chopped)

½   cup dried cranberries, currants, cherries, or chopped apricots

¼   cup pine nuts (optional)

2   teaspoons smoked paprika

¼-½   teaspoon chipotle sauce or chipotle chili powder

2-3   tablespoons breadcrumbs

   Salt and pepper, to taste

8-10   sheets phyllo dough, thawed

6-8   tablespoons olive oil for brushing phyllo

1. Heat 3 tablespoons of the oil in a large pan with lid. Add onion and garlic and sauté until onion is softened.

2. Add chard and cover pan. Heat gently until greens begin to wilt.

3. Stir in dried cranberries, pine nuts, smoked paprika, and chipotle sauce. Continue heating 5 minutes to blend flavors.

4. Stir in breadcrumbs and remaining olive oil. Season to taste with salt and pepper. Set aside to cool. May be made ahead and stored refrigerated overnight.

5. Preheat oven to 375 degrees.

6. Lightly oil a 9x9-inch pan.

7. Unwrap phyllo and place sheets on a flat surface. Cover remaining phyllo with a dry or barely damp towel. Working quickly, brush top sheet of phyllo lightly with olive oil. Place in oiled pan with sides hanging over the edge of the pan.

8. Brush next sheet with oil and place on top of first sheet. Do not worry if phyllo tears.

9. Repeat process with 2 or 3 more sheets.

10. Place greens on top of phyllo and spread evenly.

11. Fold edges of phyllo sheets over filling. Brush with oil, then layer remaining 4 sheets of phyllo dough, brushing each with oil. Tuck overhanging dough into pan to seal filling.

12. Bake in preheated oven until browned, about 30 minutes.

13. Cut into squares and serve hot.

Note: Individual servings, as pictured, can be achieved by preparing a 4-sheet layer, placing some mix in the center, and folding up four sides so they overlap at the top. Brush with oil and place seam side down on pan and bake as indicated.

huevos ahogados

These eggs have been drowned in a delicious sauce!

PARVE

2   potatoes, diced

3   tablespoons olive oil

1   onion, chopped

2-4 cloves garlic, diced

1   teaspoon smoked paprika (optional)

6   large ripe tomatoes, chopped

3-4 sun-dried tomatoes, chopped, or
     1 tablespoon tomato paste

¼-½ teaspoon hot sauce (optional)

6   eggs

     Salt, to taste

1. Boil potatoes in salted water until fork tender. Drain and set aside.

2. In a large skillet, heat oil and sauté onion and garlic until softened. Stir in smoked paprika, (if using).

3. Add tomatoes and sun-dried tomatoes or tomato paste. Simmer 30 minutes, stirring often. Add a few tablespoons water if mixture seems dry. Sauce should be thick.

4. Add potatoes and hot sauce (if using), and continue cooking 5 minutes.

5. Once potato/tomato mixture comes to a boil, make 6 wells (one at a time) and gently place 1 egg in each well, making sure not to break yolks. Do not mix!

6. Cover loosely and poach eggs for 10 minutes.

7. Serve hot over rice or toast.

desserts

desserts

chocolate cake supreme

Olive oil in chocolate cake? Sounds strange. Tastes yummy.

3   cups sugar

3   cups flour

6   eggs

1   cup olive oil

⅓   cup unsweetened applesauce

1   cup cocoa

3   teaspoons baking powder

1½ teaspoons baking soda

1   teaspoon salt

1   teaspoon vanilla extract

1¾ cups black coffee

    Toasted walnuts (optional)

1. Preheat oven to 350 degrees.

2. Lightly grease and flour an 11x17-inch pan or a Bundt pan.

3. Combine all ingredients in mixing bowl, stirring until batter is smooth.

4. Pour batter in prepared Bundt pan.

5. Bake 50 minutes in preheated oven for rectangular pan or 1 hour 10 minutes for tube pan.

6. Can also be made into cupcakes. Fill paper-lined cupcake pan ¾ full. Bake 25 minutes.

rich *and* lovely chocolate torte

DAIRY OR PARVE

This is an easy, festive, and delicious cake – it is decorated with fresh berries, and fresh flower petals can be added for an elegant touch. A great choice for a grown-up birthday cake!

10 ounces bittersweet chocolate
1 cup margarine or butter
5 large eggs
1¼ cups sugar
5 tablespoons flour
1½ teaspoons baking powder

1. Preheat oven to 325 degrees.
2. Grease and flour a 10-inch springform pan.
3. Melt chocolate and margarine either in a double boiler or in the microwave.
4. Transfer melted chocolate and margarine mixture into a mixing bowl.
5. Add eggs, one at a time, while continuously mixing batter on low speed.
6. Add sugar, flour, and baking powder and mix until ingredients are thoroughly combined.
7. Pour batter into prepared pan.
8. Bake in preheated oven for 20 minutes.
9. Remove baking pan from the oven, cover pan tightly with aluminum foil, and replace in oven for another 30 minutes.
10. Remove from oven and cool well.
11. Remove cooled cake from springform with a sharp knife, pry cake from sides of the pan, then use a long knife to gently pry cake from bottom of the pan. Flip cake onto a prepared platter so that bottom of the baked cake is now the top.
12. Gently smooth out cake with spatula and dust with confectioners' sugar.
13. Serving suggestions: Place berries, raspberries, blueberries, and sliced strawberries on and around cake. Scatter fresh rose petals on top of cake and on the surrounding platter for a dramatic presentation.

lite 'nilla cupcakes

PARVE

Light and tasty — you'd never know they're low fat and egg-free.

1   tablespoon apple cider vinegar

1½ cups almond milk or rice milk

2   cups all-purpose flour

1   cup white sugar

2   teaspoons baking powder

½   teaspoon baking soda

½   teaspoon salt

½   cup coconut oil, warmed until liquid, or
      canola oil

1¼ teaspoons vanilla extract

optional glaze:

4   cups confectioners' sugar

2   teaspoons cocoa powder

4   tablespoons orange juice

1. Preheat oven to 350 degrees.

2. Grease 2 (12 cup) muffin pans or line with 24 paper baking cups.

3. Measure apple cider vinegar and pour into a 2-cup measuring cup. Fill with almond milk to make 1½ cups. Let stand 5 minutes until curdled.

4. In a large bowl, whisk together flour, sugar, baking powder, baking soda, and salt.

5. In a separate bowl, whisk together almond milk mixture, oil, and vanilla.

6. Pour wet ingredients into dry ingredients and stir just until blended. Spoon batter into prepared cups, dividing evenly.

7. Bake in preheated oven 15-20 minutes until the tops spring back when lightly pressed.

8. Cool in pan set over a wire rack.

9. To prepare optional glaze, combine confectioners' sugar and cocoa powder in a large bowl. Add orange juice by the tablespoonful, stirring thoroughly between additions, until desired consistency. Drizzle cupcakes with glaze at least 30 minutes before serving to allow glaze to set.

fruit tart

This can become your "go-to" dessert – very easy, pretty, and tasty. Works with winter or summer fruit, so make it your own.

batter:

1 cup sugar

½ cup canola oil

1 cup unbleached flour

1 teaspoon baking powder

2 eggs

Dash salt

Fruit: 1 Granny Smith apple, 1 ripe Bosc pear, 1 ripe peach, or ½ cup blueberries — enough to cover surface of batter

topping:

4-5 tablespoons sugar

1 teaspoon cinnamon

3 tablespoons fresh-squeezed lemon juice

1. Lightly grease a 9- or 10-inch springform pan.

2. Preheat oven to 350 degrees.

3. Using a mixer, combine all ingredients for batter until completely integrated. Pour into springform pan.

4. Slice fruit thinly; do not peel. Place fruit carefully on top of batter, in a concentric circle, starting from the center. If using blueberries, cover batter with berries.

5. Sprinkle fruit with sugar and cinnamon, and spoon lemon juice on top.

6. Bake in preheated oven for 1 hour. Best served the same day plain or with whipped cream or ice cream. Tart does not freeze well.

velveteen cupcakes *with* cream cheese frosting

Trendy or not, these red velvet cakes are timelessly beautiful and delectable.

1½ cups (3 sticks) unsalted butter or margarine, softened

2 cups sugar

3 large eggs, at room temperature

3 tablespoons unsweetened cocoa

1½ teaspoons vanilla extract

6 tablespoons red food coloring

1½ teaspoons salt

1½ cups buttermilk (parve substitute: 1½ cups rice, soy, almond, or other milk substitute plus 1½ teaspoons vinegar or lemon juice)

3½ cups cake flour or 3⅓ cups unbleached flour, sifted

1½ teaspoons vinegar (cider or balsamic)

1½ teaspoons baking soda

1. Preheat oven to 350 degrees.

2. Line 2 cupcake pans with paper liners (18-24).

3. In a large bowl, on medium speed of an electric mixer, cream butter or margarine and sugar 5 minutes until light and fluffy.

4. Add eggs, one at a time, beating well after each addition.

5. Add cocoa, vanilla, and red food color and beat well.

6. In a measuring cup, stir salt into buttermilk or parve substitute. Add buttermilk to batter in 3 parts, alternating with flour. With each addition, beat until ingredients are incorporated, but do not overbeat.

7. In a small bowl, stir together cider vinegar and baking soda. Add to the batter and mix well. Using a rubber spatula, scrape down batter from sides of the bowl, making sure ingredients are well blended and batter is smooth.

8. Pour batter into cupcake liners.

9. Bake cupcakes in preheated oven for 18-20 minutes, or until tester comes out clean.

10. Let cupcakes cool in pans for at least 30 minutes. Remove from pans and cool completely on a wire rack.

11. While batter bakes, prepare the frosting.

cream cheese frosting:

3 (8 ounce) packages cream cheese
   or non-dairy cream cheese, room
   temperature

1½ sticks butter or margarine

2 cups confectioners' sugar

3 teaspoons lemon juice or
   1 teaspoon vanilla extract

   Pinch salt

1. Beat cream cheese, butter or margarine, and
   vanilla or lemon juice in medium bowl until
   smooth.

2. Beat in enough confectioners' sugar to make
   a stiff spreadable frosting. Add a few drops of
   water or milk if too stiff.

3. Spread or pipe frosting onto cooled cupcakes,
   leaving ½-inch plain border.

*Note: This recipe makes enough frosting for
36 cupcakes.*

caramel coconut flan

DAIRY

Scrumptious. An elegant and luscious alternative to cheesecake for dairy holiday meals. Traditional Spanish flan is made without coconut so you can omit here, but it adds a novel twist to a classic. Can be made in individual ramekins.

2½ cups finely grated sweetened coconut plus extra for garnish

8   eggs

2   cups sugar, divided

3   cups whole milk

3   tablespoons flour

1. Preheat oven to 325 degrees.

2. Toast coconut on baking sheet for 10-12 minutes. Cool coconut slightly and place in food processor until finely ground.

3. Increase oven to 375 degrees.

4. Whisk eggs and add 1 cup of the sugar, milk, flour, and toasted coconut, mixing well. Set aside.

5. In a heavy frying pan, melt remaining cup of sugar over medium heat. Do not stir. Swirl pan until sugar caramelizes, turning a nutty golden brown. Be careful not to let sugar burn or turn dark brown. Quickly and carefully pour melted sugar into an 8-inch cake pan, working fast — as soon as you remove pan from heat, sugar will harden. Quickly swirl caramel around to coat bottom and sides of pan.

6. Pour custard mixture on top of prepared caramel.

7. Place custard pan in larger deep-sided pan. Add boiling water to outer pan until water comes halfway up the sides of custard pan.

8. Bake in preheated oven until set and skewer comes out clean, about 55-65 minutes.

9. Remove custard pan from water bath. Allow flan to rest for 10 minutes. While still hot, invert pan onto a serving dish. Caramel will cover top and pool around flan. Garnish with reserved grated coconut.

viennese linzertorte

DAIRY OR PARVE

Beautiful and delicious — a special dessert for a special occasion.

1¾ sticks butter or margarine (unsalted) at room temperature

1 cup sugar

½ teaspoon cinnamon

1¼ cups flour (self-rising or all-purpose)

2 large egg yolks, beaten lightly

¾ teaspoon vanilla extract

1½ cups ground walnuts, filberts, or almonds

1 tablespoon fresh lemon juice

1 cup preserves (raspberry, apricot, or half of each)

1 egg white for glaze

1. Beat butter or margarine and sugar with a mixer at high speed.

2. In a separate bowl mix cinnamon and flour.

3. Pour in egg yolks and vanilla into the butter/margarine mixture and beat well. Slowly add flour to the mixing bowl and mix at low speed.

4. Mix in ground walnuts and lemon juice; mix until dough forms into a ball.

5. Wrap in a plastic bag and place in refrigerator at least 1 hour (can be made in advance and left in refrigerator overnight).

to assemble tart:

1. Preheat oven to 325 degrees.

2. Remove dough from refrigerator 10 minutes before starting to prepare. Grease a 9-inch springform pan (sides and bottom). Take ⅔ of the dough and press into prepared pan; it should be a little higher on the sides.

3. Spread preserves, leaving a ½-inch border.

4. Take smaller portion of dough; roll into a 9x8-inch rectangle. Cut 8 (1-inch-wide) strips. Place 4 strips horizontally across top of the tart. Place remaining 4 strips vertically to form a lattice top. Make sure that there are windows of jam sticking out.

5. Brush dough on top and sides with egg white.

6. Bake about 30 minutes in preheated oven until firm to touch.

7. Cool and loosen sides with a knife; take out of springform pan. Ease bottom of linzertorte with a spatula and place on cake platter.

blueberry orange bundt cake

Egg-free. A fabulous cake to make even when your guests can eat eggs — it's beautiful, flavorful, and a little zesty.

¼ cup silken tofu

½ cup water

¾ cup fresh orange juice

½ cup canola oil

1 teaspoon lemon extract

2½ cups flour

1 cup sugar

1½ teaspoons baking soda

½ teaspoon salt

Zest of 1 orange or 1 lemon

1 cup blueberries, fresh or frozen

glaze:

2 cups confectioners' sugar, sifted

Zest and juice of 2 oranges

1. Preheat oven to 350 degrees.

2. Lightly oil Bundt pan.

3. In a blender combine tofu, water, orange juice, oil, and extract; blend until smooth.

4. In a separate bowl, combine flour, sugar, baking soda, salt, and zest. Pour dry ingredients into wet. Stir until combined. Do not overmix. Fold in blueberries.

5. Pour batter into Bundt pan. Bake 50-60 minutes in preheated oven.

6. To prepare glaze, mix ingredients and pour over cooled cake. Garnish with fresh orange slices and blueberries.

Variation: Use vanilla or almond extract in place of lemon extract and leave out orange zest for a subtly different flavor.

citrus olive oil cake *with* lemon glaze

This unusual cake is like eating lemon meringue pie in a cake.

¾ cup olive oil (extra-virgin if desired), plus additional for greasing pan

Zest and juice of 1 large lemon

1 cup flour

5 large eggs, separated, reserving 1 white for another use

¾ cup plus 1½ tablespoons sugar

½ teaspoon salt

glaze:

1 cup confectioners' sugar

2 tablespoons fresh lemon juice

1. Move oven rack to middle position and preheat oven to 350 degrees.

2. Grease a springform pan with olive oil, then line bottom with a round of parchment paper. Oil parchment.

3. In a bowl, whisk lemon zest with flour.

4. Beat together yolks and ½ cup sugar in a large bowl with an electric mixer at high speed until thick and pale, about 3 minutes. Reduce speed to medium and add olive oil (¾ cup) and juice of 1 lemon, beating until just combined (mixture may appear separated).

5. Stir in flour mixture (do not beat) until just combined.

6. Beat egg whites (from 4 eggs) with salt in another large bowl with cleaned beaters at medium-high speed until foamy, then add ¼ cup of the sugar a little at a time, beating, and continue to beat until egg whites just hold soft peaks. Gently fold ⅓ of the whites into yolk mixture to lighten; fold in remaining whites gently but thoroughly.

7. Transfer batter to springform pan and gently tap against work surface once or twice to release any air bubbles. Sprinkle top evenly with remaining 1½ tablespoons sugar.

8. Bake about 45 minutes, until puffed and golden and a tester inserted in center of cake comes out clean.

9. To prepare glaze, mix sugar and fresh lemon juice; pour mixture over cooled cake to coat.

chocolate date squares

DAIRY OR PARVE

The dates add a surprisingly rich flavor to the chocolate.

2½ squares unsweetened chocolate

⅔ cup hot water

1⅓ cups granulated sugar

1⅓ cups chopped dates

1 cup butter or margarine, divided

1 teaspoon vanilla extract

1¼ cups brown sugar

1½ cups flour

½ teaspoon salt

½ teaspoon baking soda

1 cup chopped nuts

1½ cups oats

1. Preheat oven to 350 degrees.

2. To make chocolate date filling, melt chocolate in hot water, add sugar, and stir until dissolved. Add dates and cook over low heat about 5 minutes. Add ¼ cup of the butter and vanilla; cool.

3. To make crust and topping, cream remaining ¾ cup butter with brown sugar.

4. Add salt and baking soda to flour then mix into butter and brown sugar. Stir in nuts and oats; mix until crumbly.

5. Press half the oat-nut mixture into bottom of 2 greased 8-inch square pans; spread date-chocolate mixture on bottom crust and top with remaining oat-nut mixture.

6. Bake in preheated oven for 30 minutes.

chocolate mint chewies

PARVE OR DAIRY

Delicious crispy cookies.

12 ounces chocolate chips

6 tablespoons flour (can use whole wheat, pastry, white, rice, or spelt flour)

½ teaspoon baking powder

¾ cup sugar

2 eggs

2 tablespoons rice syrup or honey

½ teaspoon peppermint extract

Parchment paper

1. Preheat oven to 350 degrees.

2. In a 4 cup Pyrex measuring cup or microwavable bowl, melt chocolate chips. (Melt chips in 1-minute intervals to prevent chips from burning.) Stir until smooth.

3. Add flour and baking powder; stir.

4. Add sugar, eggs, rice syrup or honey, and peppermint extract. Stir until mixed.

5. Place sheet of parchment paper on cookie sheet. Spoon out batter, leaving 1 inch between cookies.

6. Bake for 10-12 minutes. Cookies will be soft, but set. Leave cookies on parchment (but not on cookie sheet) for 15 minutes to cool.

7. Store in container.

lime bars

PARVE OR DAIRY

A simple variation on lemon bars with a less tart, more subtle citrus flavor.

crust:

½ cup brown sugar

Pinch salt

2 cups sifted all-purpose flour

1½ sticks butter or margarine

filling:

1½ cups superfine sugar (or regular granulated)

4 eggs

6 tablespoons freshly squeezed lime juice (from 4-5 limes)

2 tablespoons lime zest (from 4-5 limes)

¼ cup unbleached, all-purpose flour

½ teaspoon baking powder

Pinch salt

1 tablespoon confectioners' sugar

1. Preheat oven to 350 degrees. Line a 9x13-inch baking pan with a strip of parchment paper or aluminum foil that covers bottom and overlaps on both sides.

2. To prepare crust, place dry ingredients into the bowl of food processor and pulse to mix. Add butter, cut into small pieces, and pulse until the mixture resembles very coarse meal or crumbs.

3. Spread crust mixture evenly on the prepared pan, and pat it down so that it makes a smooth, even layer. Place crust in preheated oven and bake for 10 minutes until crust is set. Remove from oven.

4. To prepare filling, whisk ingredients except for confectioners' sugar in a large bowl. Pour into partially baked crust.

5. Bake for 30 minutes until filling is completely set but not dry.

6. Let cool completely. (May be placed in the freezer for about 1 hour.) While holding overlapping edges of parchment paper, gently lift dessert from the pan. Cut into squares.

7. Dust with confectioners' sugar.

Variation: Can be made in a tart pan for a more formal presentation. For an added touch, decorate with sliced limes dipped in sugar.

fruit *and* oat snack bars

A great homemade granola bars.

- 2 cups old-fashioned oats
- ½ cup assorted unsalted seeds (pumpkin, sunflower, sesame)
- 1 cup dried fruit (raisins, cherries, blueberries, and/or chopped apricots)
- ¼ teaspoon ground cardamom
- 1 teaspoon cinnamon
- 6 tablespoons safflower or canola oil, plus a little more to brush the parchment paper
- ⅓ cup dark brown sugar
- ½ cup honey
- ⅓ cup maple syrup
- Salt, to taste

1. Preheat oven to 350 degrees.

2. Place parchment paper or foil into a 9-inch square pan, allowing a couple of inches to extend over sides of the pan. Brush paper with oil.

3. Spread oats and seeds in a single layer on a jelly-roll sheet and roast 5 minutes.

4. Mix oats, seeds, and dried fruit with cardamom and cinnamon in a medium-sized mixing bowl.

5. Combine oil, sugar, honey, syrup, and salt in a medium-sized saucepan. Stir over medium heat until mixture is smooth and hot.

6. Pour hot mixture over oat mixture and stir until well combined.

7. Transfer to 9-inch pan. Using a spatula, press mixture evenly into the pan.

8. Bake in preheated oven 30-45 minutes; remove when top is golden brown. Transfer pan to a rack and cool.

9. While holding overlapping edges of foil or paper, lift mixture out of the pan and place on flat surface. When completely cool cut into individual bars.

egg-free lemon mousse

DAIRY OR PARVE

Whether you have egg allergies or are just watching your cholesterol, this is a delicious option.

¾ cup fresh lemon juice

¼ cup water

   Zest of 1 lemon

6 tablespoons sugar

3 tablespoons cornstarch or potato starch

⅛ teaspoon or pinch turmeric (for color)

1 tablespoon margarine or butter

¼ teaspoon lemon extract

¾ teaspoon vanilla extract, divided

1 cup whipping cream or parve whipped topping

2 tablespoons confectioners' sugar

1. Whisk lemon juice, water, zest, sugar, starch, turmeric, and margarine in saucepan.

2. Heat until mixture simmers, whisking constantly. Custard will thicken dramatically.

3. Continue cooking for 1-2 minutes, stirring to prevent scorching.

4. Remove from heat and stir in lemon extract and ¼ teaspoon vanilla extract.

5. Transfer custard to a bowl and cool in refrigerator for at least 1 hour. (May be made 1-2 days ahead.)

6. Whip cream until starts to thicken. Add sugar and remaining vanilla. Continue beating until soft peaks form. If using parve whipped topping, omit confectioners' sugar.

7. Fold whipped cream into cooled custard.

8. Transfer to a serving bowl and refrigerate until firm. Mousse may be frozen for a different texture.

lemon mousse

PARVE OR DAIRY

The most delicious non-chocolate mousse you will have, and simple to make too!

¾ cup sugar

⅛ teaspoon salt

2 tablespoons kudzu starch, cornstarch, or potato starch

Zest of 1 lemon

¼ cup water

¾ cup fresh lemon juice, strained

3 yolks or 1 large egg plus 1 yolk

1 tablespoon butter, margarine, or coconut oil

1¼ teaspoons vanilla extract, divided

½ teaspoon lemon extract

2 cups whipping cream or 1 large carton parve whipped cream

3 tablespoons confectioners' sugar, if using heavy cream

1. Whisk sugar, salt, starch, lemon zest, water, lemon juice, and eggs in a medium saucepan. Cook over medium heat, whisking constantly, until mixture simmers and thickens dramatically.

2. Reduce heat and continue cooking for about 1 minute, stirring to prevent scorching. Stir in butter.

3. Remove from heat and stir in 1 teaspoon of the vanilla extract and the lemon extract.

4. Strain custard through a fine mesh strainer into a large bowl, scraping with a spoon or rubber spatula (optional, but makes mousse smoother and more elegant).

5. Cover and let lemon custard cool in the refrigerator. May be stored in the refrigerator for several days.

6. Whip cream until it begins to thicken. Add confectioners' sugar and remaining vanilla once cream begins to thicken. Continue beating until cream forms soft peaks. If using parve topping, omit sugar, beat until soft peaks form and stir in vanilla.

7. Fold whipped cream into lemon custard. Transfer to a large serving bowl or individual ramekins.

8. Cover and store in refrigerator until mousse sets. May be frozen for a different texture.

raspberry or strawberry mousse variation:

1 cup raspberries or strawberries or mixture of both

1 tablespoon cornstarch or potato starch

2 tablespoons confectioners' sugar

Pinch salt

1 tablespoon raspberry syrup or pomegranate molasses

2 cups whipping cream or parve whipped topping

1 recipe cold lemon custard, made without lemon zest or lemon extract

1. Purée berries with starch, sugar, salt, and syrup in a food processor or with an immersion blender.

2. Strain berry mixture through a fine mesh strainer to remove seeds. Set berries aside (maybe stored overnight refrigerated).

3. Whip cream until firm peaks.

4. Remove cooled lemon custard from refrigerator and fold in whipped cream.

5. Gently fold berry mixture into mousse.

6. Transfer to a decorative bowl or individual dishes. Place mousse in refrigerator for several hours or overnight until firm. Mousse may be frozen for a different texture.

watermelon granita

Light and refreshing, this is an ideal dessert for summer barbecues.

¾　cup water

¾　cup sugar

8　cups watermelon, seeded and chunked
　　(1-2 small watermelons)

　　Juice of 2-3 limes

½　teaspoon salt

1. Make simple syrup by heating water and sugar in a saucepan just until sugar dissolves. Alternately, sugar and water may be heated in a microwave until sugar has dissolved. Cool simple syrup until room temperature (may be stored in refrigerator for 1-2 weeks).

2. Purée watermelon in a food processor until smooth. Watermelon may be strained through a fine mesh strainer if desired.

3. Mix simple syrup, lime juice, and salt into watermelon.

4. Pour mixture into an 11x13-inch baking pan and freeze for 6 hours, scraping mixture every 2-3 hours with a fork (optional but more authentic).

5. Serve by scraping icy watermelon treat into bowls.

Optional: To create a smoother more sorbet-like texture, purée watermelon in a food processor every 2-3 hours instead of scraping with a fork.

lemon-basil granita

PARVE

Cool, refreshing and elegant dessert for hot summer daytime meals. Feel free to vary the citrus fruit. Oranges or limes or a mixture would be a great alternative.

4   lemons

¼-⅓ cup fresh basil (or mint, or a mix of both)

4   cups water

3-6 tablespoons sugar, divided

1. Wash lemons and slice into quarters lengthwise. Carefully remove all lemon flesh and juice over a large bowl using a sharp paring knife.

2. Using a food processor or blender, combine basil or mint and the scooped out lemon flesh and juice; pulse until mostly puréed. Let mixture stand for 15 minutes, then press mixture through a fine-mesh strainer. The final volume should be approximately 1 cup of lemon-mint juice.

3. Mix water and 3 tablespoons of the sugar in a measuring cup until sugar is dissolved. Stir sugar/water into lemon mixture. Adjust sweetness by adding 1 tablespoon of the sugar at a time. Mixture should be sweet, but refreshingly tart.

4. Pour mixture into a large roasting pan or 9x13-inch baking dish.

5. Freeze for 3 hours, scraping it with forks every hour or so until mixture is frozen.

6. When granita is frozen, scrape until glittery to serve.

7. Garnish with fresh raspberries and a drizzle of reduced balsamic vinegar.

white *and* dark chocolate bark

A dramatic and delicious addition to any dessert table. Simple and sophisticated. Feel free to create your own variations.

3 cups pecan halves, or 2 cups filberts and 1 cup dried cherries, or 2 cups almonds and 1 cup raisins

16 ounces white chocolate, chopped into ¼-inch pieces

24 ounces semisweet chocolate, chopped into ¼-inch pieces

1. Preheat oven to 325 degrees.

2. Toast nuts on a baking sheet in preheated oven for 8 minutes, or until nuts are lightly browned and fragrant.

3. Remove nuts from oven and set aside to cool to room temperature until needed.

4. Melt white chocolate in a double boiler, stirring until chocolate is completely melted and smooth. Transfer melted white chocolate to a 1-quart bowl and set aside.

5. Wash and dry double boiler and repeat with semisweet chocolate.

6. Alternately, melt white and semisweet chocolate, separately, in a microwave at full power in 10-20 second intervals until chocolate has softened. Stir well until chocolate is smooth and shiny. Allow chocolate to stand at room temperature for 5 minutes before proceeding.

7. Fold nuts and fruit into semisweet chocolate until combined. Pour chocolate pecan mixture onto a nonstick baking sheet with sides lined with parchment, wax paper, or foil. Spread evenly with a rubber spatula.

8. Drizzle white chocolate, 1 tablespoon at a time, over entire surface of the chocolate pecan mixture. Use a rubber spatula to spread and blend white chocolate into surface of the chocolate pecan mixture, creating a marbleized effect (be careful not to over blend to keep the marbleized effect). Allow mixture to set at room temperature for 30 minutes.

9. Cover the baking sheet with plastic wrap and refrigerate about 1 hour until bark is hard.

10. Remove baking sheet from the refrigerator and transfer bark to a cutting board. Use a cook's knife to cut bark into irregular pieces.

11. Refrigerate in a tightly sealed plastic container until ready to use.

trio of hot beverages

A great end to a winter meal, either with or instead of dessert.

warm apple cider:

PARVE

Gallon of apple cider

2 cups orange juice

1 tablespoon nutmeg

1 tablespoon cinnamon or 5 cinnamon sticks

1. Place ingredients in hot water urn. Alternatively, apple cider may be warmed in a crockpot on low for 2-3 hours.

white hot cocoa:

DAIRY

1 cup white chocolate, broken into pieces (chips may be substituted)

1 cup cream

4 cups whole milk

1 teaspoon vanilla extract

1. In a saucepan heat together cream and chips until chips melt. Then stir in vanilla and milk.

chai tea:

DAIRY OR PARVE

10 whole green cardamom pods, lightly crushed

5 whole cloves

2 cinnamon sticks

1 piece fresh ginger (about 2 inches), peeled and quartered

½ vanilla bean, split lengthwise and scraped

⅓ cup honey, plus more for serving (optional)

4 bags unflavored tea (such as English Breakfast, Ceylon, or black tea)

1½ cups milk (or almond milk)

1. Place 3 cups water in a small saucepan and add cardamom, cloves, cinnamon, ginger, and vanilla bean including scrapings. Bring to a boil over high heat.

2. Reduce heat to low; simmer uncovered until mixture is aromatic, about 15 minutes.

3. Whisk in honey until dissolved.

4. Drop tea bags in pan and turn off heat. Steep tea for 3 minutes.

5. Strain tea through a fine strainer or a coffee filter into a warmed serving pot.

6. Heat milk in same saucepan over medium-high heat for about 3 minutes without letting it boil.

7. Pour into serving pot with tea, and stir well to combine. Serve immediately, with more honey on the side if desired.

caramel popcorn

PARVE OR DAIRY

Making your own caramel popcorn is a whole new snacking experience. Both the dairy and parve versions are great, but the dairy is a rich special treat.

10 cups freshly popped corn

2 cups brown sugar

½ cup butter or margarine

½ cup corn syrup, rice syrup, or mixture of honey and maple syrup

1 teaspoon salt

1 teaspoon baking soda

1. Preheat oven to 200 degrees.

2. Spread popcorn onto 2 or 3 large pans with sides.

3. In a saucepan, mix brown sugar, margarine or butter, syrup, and salt. Heat, stirring gently, until mixture simmers. Continue to cook for 5 minutes.

4. Remove pan from heat and add baking soda, stirring vigorously. Sugar mixture will bubble up dramatically and change to a light caramel color.

5. Quickly pour over popcorn, distributing as evenly as possible between the 2 or 3 pans.

6. Mix popcorn to coat with caramel as quickly as possible.

7. Place pans in oven for 30 minutes, stirring every 10-15 minutes.

8. Remove from oven and cool to room temperature. Store in sealed containers at room temperature.

shabbat and holiday

bubbie's challah

PARVE

A delicious classic that's tried and true. The recipe makes 8 loaves.

4   packages yeast

4   cups warm water

1   teaspoon sugar

5   pounds (1 bag) plus 1 cup bread flour, divided

2   cups sugar

2   tablespoons salt

1½ cups canola oil

8   eggs, beaten

2   eggs, beaten, for coating

1. Combine yeast, warm water, and 1 teaspoon sugar in a bowl and set aside for 10 minutes to proof.

2. Mix 5 pounds of the flour, sugar, and salt in a large bowl. Make a well in the center and add oil, 8 eggs, and proofed yeast mixture. Mix dough with a spoon or with your hands until dough comes together in a mass.

3. Transfer to a well-floured board and knead for 10 minutes until dough is smooth and pliable, adding remaining cup of flour gradually to prevent sticking.

4. Place kneaded dough in oiled bowl. Cover with plastic wrap and a towel. Let dough rise overnight in refrigerator.

5. Punch down and let dough rise again at room temperature until doubled, about 2 hours.

6. Preheat oven to 350 degrees.

7. Punch down, cut into 8 pieces, and shape or braid each piece into a challah loaf.

8. Place loaves on lightly oiled baking sheets spaced 2 inches apart. Let rise for 30 minutes at room temperature until puffy. Brush with remaining beaten 2 eggs.

9. Bake in preheated oven for 30 minutes. Cool on racks.

10. This recipe is large enough to take challah and make a bracha.

Note: *Recipe may be cut in half to make 3-4 loaves, using 6-8 cups flour.*

honey whole wheat challah

A more healthful version of the classic challah that delivers on taste and texture. Makes four pull-apart challahs.

2   packages quick-acting yeast

2   cups warm water

1   heaping tablespoon salt

¾   cup honey

2½ cups white wheat flour

2   eggs

½   cup canola oil

5½ cups bread flour or high gluten white flour

½   cup sesame or poppy seeds (optional)

1. Place yeast in mixing bowl of a mixer fitted with a dough hook. With machine on low speed, stir in warm water, salt, and honey until thoroughly mixed.

2. Add 2½ cups wheat flour. Next, mix in eggs and oil until combined.

3. Add white flour 2 cups at a time. Continue mixing until dough is smooth and slightly sticky. If dough is too wet, add a small amount of flour.

4. Transfer dough to a floured board and knead for about 1 minute, until dough is smooth.

5. Liberally oil a large glass or metal bowl. Place dough in oiled bowl and cover with a large greased piece of plastic wrap. Cover bowl with a towel and let rise at least 2 hours at room temperature.

6. Preheat oven to 350 degrees.

7. To shape challah, divide dough into 24 pieces. Form each piece into a ball, about 2 inches in diameter. This recipe makes 4 pull-apart challahs.

8. Lightly oil 4 (8-inch) round pans. Place 6 balls into each pan — 1 ball in the center and 5 balls surrounding. Make sure dough does not overflow edge of the pans.

9. Let challah rise about 2 hours. Brush challah with egg wash and sprinkle with sesame seeds and/or poppy seeds, if desired.

10. Bake preheated oven for 35-40 minutes.

11. Let cool for about 30 minutes. Remove from pan.

i-can't-believe-it's-water challah

PARVE

A recipe that is sure to fool even the staunchest water-challah skeptics. Makes four loaves.

1   tablespoon yeast

3   tablespoons sugar

1   cup warm water

8   cups flour

1   tablespoon baking powder

1   teaspoon salt

2   cups hot water

½   cup olive oil, plus more if needed

1   egg, plus 1 tablespoon water, beaten for glaze

1. Mix yeast, sugar, and warm water with a fork in a small bowl and sprinkle a little flour on top (yeast should bubble and rise when you do this).

2. Place flour, baking powder, salt, and hot water in a large bowl or a mixer fit with a dough hook.

3. Turn mixer on to low-medium speed. Gradually pour in oil while mixing. Then add in yeast mixture and mix (either with mixer or by hand) until dough comes together. Continue kneading dough until smooth.

4. Transfer to a lightly oiled bowl and cover with plastic wrap. Let dough rise in a large bowl for about 1 hour. Punch dough down and knead 1-2 tablespoons oil into dough.

5. Divide dough into 4 pieces. Form loaves as desired and place onto greased baking sheets.

6. Let dough rise again for about 1 hour until puffy. Brush with egg wash.

7. Bake at 350 degrees for about 20 minutes until challahs have some color on top.

cardamom challah

PARVE

We were all a bit doubtful about cardamom in challah, but this recipe was a unanimous hit. A must-try recipe! Makes 2 loaves.

1   envelope instant yeast

¾   cup warm water

¼   cup sugar plus 2 tablespoons, divided

3¾ cups bread flour

2   large eggs

½   cup vegetable oil

1½ teaspoons kosher salt

½   teaspoon ground cardamom

1   egg plus 1 teaspoon water, beaten for glaze

1. Mix yeast, warm water, and 2 tablespoons of the sugar in a small bowl or measuring cup and set aside for 5 minutes to proof.

2. Add remaining ingredients to bowl of mixer fitted with a dough hook. Knead until dough is smooth and firm, adding more flour if necessary.

3. Transfer dough to a lightly oiled bowl and cover with plastic wrap. Let dough rise in a warm place about 2 hours, until doubled in bulk.

4. Punch down and divide dough into 2 pieces. Shape dough and place on 2 parchment-lined cookie sheets. Allow to rise about 1 hour until doubled in bulk.

5. Brush challah with egg glaze and bake at 350 degrees for about 25-35 minutes.

holiday gefilte fish

If you ever wondered if making your own gefilte fish is worth the effort, this recipe will surely convince you. A simple recipe with delicious results.

2   pounds white fish plus 1 pound pike, ground

1¼ cups sugar

2   tablespoons salt

1   tablespoon white pepper

1   large onion, grated

2-4 large carrots, peeled and grated

3   eggs

1   cup matzo meal

2   carrots, cleaned and sliced in half lengthwise

for cooking frozen loaves:

2   onions, thickly sliced

2   carrots, large chunks

1   cup sugar

2-3 cups water

   Salt and pepper, to taste

1. Preheat oven to 350 degrees.

2. Thoroughly mix first 8 ingredients by hand in a large bowl. Mixture will be soft and pasty.

3. Line 3 loaf pans with parchment paper hanging over sides.

4. Fill halfway with fish mixture. Place peeled and trimmed carrot halves along the center in a single line. Fill loaf pans with remaining fish mixture, covering carrot. Using overhang of parchment, wrap up fish loaf. Cover pan with aluminum foil, sealing tightly.

5. Place on a foil- or parchment-lined baking sheet, to catch drips.

6. Bake in preheated oven for 1½ hours.

7. Cool loaves in pan. Refrigerate several hours or overnight before slicing and serving.

8. Alternatively, freeze loaves, wrapped in parchment. When ready to cook, place frozen loaves in parchment in a large pan with onions, carrots, sugar, salt and pepper. Add water. Cover pot and bring to a boil. Reduce heat to a simmer and continue cooking gently for 1½ hours. Remove loaves from broth along with onions and carrots to cool. Refrigerate several hours or overnight before unwrapping to slice and serve.

fassoulyeh b'lah'meh *(syrian cholent)*

MEAT

An interesting variation on a Shabbat staple.

1 pound great white Northern beans

1 cup thinly sliced onions

2 tablespoons olive oil

Pinch saffron (optional)

3 pounds flanken meat

½ cup white flour, for dredging

2-3 cloves garlic

5 cups water

1 can (6 ounce) tomato paste

1 teaspoon cinnamon

1 teaspoon allspice

2 tablespoons sugar

2 teaspoons salt

Pepper, to taste

1. Soak beans for 6-10 hours. Drain and set aside until needed.

2. Heat oil in a large pan. Sauté onions with saffron (if using) until golden. Remove with a spoon, leaving oil in the pan.

3. Dredge flanken in flour and brown on both sides in the same pan used to sauté onions.

4. Place flanken on the bottom of a 5- or 6-quart crockpot. Cover with sautéed onions, garlic, and soaked beans.

5. Mix water, tomato paste, cinnamon, allspice, sugar, salt, and pepper; add to the crockpot without stirring beans and meat.

6. Cook on low in crockpot overnight.

shabbat morning potato kugel

PARVE

The ultimate comfort food that will fill your home with the unmistakable aromas of Shabbat.

½ cup oil, plus 2 tablespoons

4 onions, thinly sliced

1-2 tablespoons salt, divided

7 eggs

1 teaspoon black pepper

White pepper, to taste

5 pounds potatoes, peeled and quartered

3 pounds flanken

1 cup water

1. Heat 2 tablespoons of the oil in large frying pan over medium heat. Add onions and ½ teaspoon of the salt. Sauté about 30 minutes, until caramelized.

2. Preheat oven to 400 degrees.

3. Pour oil into large roasting pan and place in oven.

4. Whisk eggs, onions, and spices in large bowl and set aside. Use a food processor to shred or grate potatoes in several batches. Quickly add each batch to egg mixture.

5. Season flanken to taste with salt and pepper. Carefully, lay flanken in single layer in pan of hot oil.

6. Pour potato mixture over flanken.

7. Bake uncovered in preheated oven for 30 minutes.

8. Reduce heat to 350 degrees and cook for 1 hour.

9. Pour water over kugel; cover tightly and reduce heat to 200 degrees.

10. Bake overnight for up to 18-24 hours.

yerushalmi kugel

A traditional dish that is the perfect mix of sweet and savory.

16 ounces fine noodles or 1 box angel hair pasta

4 eggs or 8 egg whites

2¼ cups sugar, divided

1½ teaspoons salt

1½ teaspoons pepper

1 heaping teaspoon cinnamon

½ cup oil

1. Cook pasta according to package directions, then drain.

2. Mix eggs, 1½ cups sugar, salt, pepper, and cinnamon in a large bowl; add cooked noodles.

3. Preheat oven to 350 degrees.

4. In a medium pot, heat oil and ¾ cup sugar on medium heat until sugar begins to brown; reduce heat to low. Cook until sugar is an amber color and caramelized. Be careful not to burn sugar.

5. After sugar caramelizes, remove it from the flame and add pasta mixture into the pot with sugar. If sugar crystallizes, then place the pot with all ingredients back on the heat until sugar returns to a liquid again.

6. Pour the contents of the pot into a 9x13-inch pan.

7. Bake covered in preheated oven for 45 minutes and uncovered for an additional 25 minutes.

sour cream coffee cake

The perfect cake for Shabbat morning coffee and tea!

DAIRY OR PARVE

½   cup sugar

½   cup brown sugar

½   cup butter or margarine

2   eggs

1   teaspoon vanilla extract

2½ cups flour

1½ teaspoons baking powder

1   teaspoon baking soda

¼   teaspoon salt

1½ cups sour cream or parve sour cream

topping *and* filling:

½   cup sugar

1   tablespoon brown sugar

2   tablespoons cocoa

2   teaspoons cinnamon

    Heaping ½ cup chocolate chips

alternate topping *and* filling:

½   cup chocolate or white chocolate chips (optional)

⅓   cup brown sugar

⅓   cup oats

3   tablespoons butter or margarine, melted and cooled

    Pinch salt

2   teaspoons cinnamon

½   cup pecans or walnuts, chopped and toasted (optional)

1. Preheat oven to 350 degrees.

2. Lightly grease a Bundt pan or tube pan.

3. Cream sugars and butter until light.

4. Add eggs and vanilla; combine well.

5. Combine flour, baking powder, baking soda, and salt.

6. Add flour mixture and sour cream to creamed mixture in 2 or 3 additions, mixing well after each.

7. To prepare topping and filling, combine ingredients in a small bowl.

8. Spread ½ of the cake batter into a prepared Bundt pan. Sprinkle with ⅔ of the topping. Spread the remaining batter over filling and sprinkle top with the remaining topping.

9. Bake for approximately 45-50 minutes, or until a toothpick comes out clean.

10. Cool in the pan on a rack for approximately 20 minutes. Remove from pan to cool completely.

tzibbele kichel

If you could cross the classic onion roll with a flat pita bread you would have tzibbele kichel. An ideal bread for a Shalosh Seudot meal or to dip in hummus or guacamole.

¾ cup oil

2 large onions, finely chopped

Salt and pepper, to taste

2 eggs

4 cups flour

2 tablespoons sugar

2 tablespoons poppy seeds

2½ teaspoons baking powder

1. Heat 2 tablespoons oil in skillet over medium-high heat.

2. Sauté onions until translucent and soft. Season to taste with salt and pepper if desired. Combine with remaining ingredients until crumbly. Mix in onions until evenly distributed.

3. Form dough into 2 discs, wrap in plastic wrap, and place in refrigerator for 30 minutes to overnight.

4. Roll out dough to ¼ inch thick on 2 separate baking sheets covered with parchment paper. Cover in plastic wrap and place back into refrigerator for another hour.

5. Preheat oven to 350 degrees.

6. Score dough into intersecting diagonals.

7. Bake 15-20 minutes until light brown.

rib-eye roast *with* roasted fingerling potatoes

MEAT

An exquisite recipe from the chef at New York City's famed Le Marais. A perfect entrée for a festive holiday meal or special occasion.

roast::

3   carrots, peeled and cut into large chunks

2   yellow onions, peeled and quartered

2   cups water

1   (6 pound) rib-eye roast

¾   cup red wine

2   cups beef stock

   Salt and black pepper, to taste

fingerling potatoes:

2   pounds fingerling potatoes, cleaned

2-3 tablespoons extra-virgin olive oil

4   sprigs rosemary, leaves only, finely chopped

1. Preheat oven to 450 degrees.

2. Make a bed in the roasting pan with carrots and onions. Add water. Place roast on top of vegetables and place in oven. Roast for 25 minutes, adding water to vegetables if necessary.

3. After 25 minutes, reduce the heat to 275 degrees and continue to bake for about another 45 minutes, or until internal temperature of roast reaches 130 degrees for rare.

4. Remove roast from oven. Transfer roast and vegetables to a platter and cover lightly with foil. Allow roast to rest 10-15 minutes before slicing.

5. While meat is resting, strain drippings from the pan into a cup. Skim fat from the drippings.

6. Place the roasting pan over 2 burners; heat on medium-high. Add wine and beef stock, scraping up browned bits to deglaze the pan. Stir in drippings and continue cooking about 5 minutes, until gravy is reduced by ⅓, stirring occasionally. Turn off heat; season to taste with salt and pepper. Reheat before serving.

7. Prepare potatoes before placing roast in oven. Place a roasting pan in oven while oven preheats. Cut potatoes in half, if large. Season well with salt and black pepper and then toss with extra-virgin olive oil and chopped rosemary.

8. Place potatoes in the hot pan and roast about 20 minutes until golden brown while beef roasts at 450° degrees. Remove from oven and set aside at room temperature. Reheat at 350 degrees for 10 minutes while meat rests.

chai honey cake

An aromatic honey cake perfect for Rosh Hashana but easy enough to make for a weekday snack!

4   eggs

1½ cups sugar

¾   cup oil

1   cup honey

2   teaspoons baking powder

2½ cups flour

     Pinch salt

1   cup chai spice tea, cooled

1   teaspoon baking soda

glaze (optional):

1   cup confectioners' sugar

1   tablespoon milk or water

¼   teaspoon vanilla extract

     Pinch salt

1. Preheat oven to 325 degrees.

2. Place all cake ingredients in a bowl and stir well.

3. Pour into a 9x13-inch greased pan.

4. Bake in preheated oven for 1 hour. Cool.

5. To prepare glaze, mix ingredients in a small bowl until smooth and pourable, adding confectioners' sugar or water as needed. Drizzle cooled cake with glaze before serving.

savory stuffed savoy cabbage

This dish is both beautiful and unusually flavorful and delicious.

sauce:

2   tablespoons olive oil

1   cup finely diced onion

2   cloves garlic, minced

    Pinch red pepper flakes

1   teaspoon chili powder

1   can (28 ounce) tomato purée

    Juice of 2 lemons

1   jar (13 ounce) red currant jelly

½   teaspoon kosher salt

meat filling:

1½ pounds ground beef

2   cups cooked short grain rice
    (1 cup raw)

2   eggs

1   teaspoon paprika

2   teaspoons ground celery seed

⅛   teaspoon white pepper

2   teaspoons kosher salt

1   cup grated onion

cabbage:

2   heads savoy cabbage

1   large onion, finely diced

1   tablespoon salt

1. To prepare sauce, heat oil in medium-size saucepan over medium heat. Add onion, garlic, red pepper flakes, and chili powder.

2. Cook, stirring constantly, until onion is tender, about 6 minutes. Add tomato purée, lemon juice, and currant jelly. Bring to a boil, reduce heat and simmer, stirring occasionally about 20 minutes until slightly thick.

3. Season to taste with salt and let cool completely.

4. Sauce can be refrigerated for up to 2 days or frozen.

5. To prepare meat filling, gently stir ingredients together with a fork until just combined.

6. To prepare cabbage, fill large stockpot with water and 1 tablespoon salt and bring to a boil. Place whole cabbage head, core side down, into boiling water. Boil for 5 minutes. Using large tongs, carefully remove cabbage and invert into colander to drain. When cool enough to handle, carefully remove outer layers. Return to pot of boiling water and repeat until all larger outer leaves are steamed and removed. Repeat with second head of cabbage.

7. Trim thick part of rib from outer leaves of each cabbage with a small paring knife, leaving leaf intact.

8. Alternately, freeze head of cabbage overnight. Remove from freezer and thaw at room temperature until outer leaves are easily removed. Continue thawing and removing large outer leaves.

9. Core and shred any remaining cabbage. Add shredded cabbage and diced onion to bottom of a large shallow baking dish.

10. Preheat oven to 375 degrees.

to assemble cabbage rolls:

1. Place ¼ cup of meat filling in the lower center part of a cabbage leaf. Fold core end over filling, fold in sides and roll cabbage over to form a package. Place stuffed cabbage seam side down over cabbage onion mixture in pan. Repeat with remaining leaves and filling. Spread sauce over stuffed cabbage. Cover with foil and bake in preheated oven for 2 hours.

pistachio-pomegranate wild rice salad

PARVE

A colorful and classy "salad" for any holiday meal.

salad:

4   tablespoons olive oil, divided

10 shallots or 1 large red onion, thinly sliced

    Pinch saffron

    Salt, to taste

2   cups uncooked wild rice mixture

4   cups chicken or vegetable stock

1¾ cups pomegranate seeds

1   cup shelled pistachios, lightly toasted and
      coarsely chopped

1   orange, peeled and sliced into 1-inch pieces

1   cup chopped cilantro

1   cup chopped flat-leaf parsley

dressing:

⅓   cup red wine vinegar

¼   cup olive oil

1   tablespoon orange juice

1   teaspoon honey

1. To prepare salad, heat 1 tablespoon of the olive oil over medium heat. Add shallots with saffron and salt to taste. Stir frequently 12-14 minutes until golden.

2. Remove shallots from pan; set aside. Add rice to pot; stir for 1 minute. Add stock and ½ teaspoon salt, bring to a boil, and stir again.

3. Cover and reduce heat to low simmer. Allow to cook for about 45 minutes, or as directed on rice package. Remove from heat and allow rice to cool completely. Add remaining ingredients.

4. To prepare dressing, combine red wine vinegar, olive oil, orange juice, and honey; whisk to incorporate. Pour over rice mixture.

5. Serve warm or room temperature.

a pair *of* fruity applesauces

Two tart treats that "riff" on the traditional Rosh Hashana meal staple.

rhubarb strawberry applesauce:

PARVE

4-5 cups rhubarb, cut into 1-inch pieces
    (frozen or fresh)

3-4 cups peeled, cored, and roughly chopped
    apples

1   small carton strawberries, sliced

½   cup sugar

½   cup water

    Pinch salt

    Pinch cinnamon

    Pinch cardamom (optional)

1. Combine all ingredients in a medium saucepan and bring to a boil over medium heat. Simmer for 20-30 minutes until completely softened and rhubarb pieces are falling apart.

2. Mash with a potato masher or use immersion blender to create desired consistency. Sauce should be slightly chunky.

lemony applesauce:

PARVE

1   cup evaporated cane juice or ¾ cup white
    sugar

½   cup water

    Zest and juice of 1 lemon

5   pears, peeled, cored, and roughly chopped

10 apples, peeled, cored, and roughly chopped

1. Mix sugar, water, lemon zest, and juice in pot.

2. Bring to a boil, then simmer. Add pears and cook for 10 minutes. Add apples and simmer covered for 1 hour, stirring occasionally until fruit has broken down.

3. Mash with potato masher or use immersion blender to create desired consistency.

large parmesan potato latke

DAIRY

Once you try this dish, you won't want to wait for Chanuka to serve it.

3   tablespoons olive oil, divided

2   leeks, sliced, soaked, and drained

1   clove garlic, minced

2   pounds Yukon gold potatoes, peeled

1   cup grated Parmesan cheese

    Salt and freshly ground black pepper, to taste

1. Warm 2 tablespoons of the olive oil in a large 12-inch nonstick pan over medium-high heat. Add leeks and cook about 6 minutes until translucent. Add garlic and cook until tender and fragrant, about another 2 minutes.

2. Season leek mixture to taste with salt and pepper. Transfer leek mixture to a large bowl and set aside. Reserve the pan.

3. Meanwhile, grate potatoes in a food processor.

4. Use a kitchen towel to help squeeze out water from the grated potatoes. Add potatoes to the bowl with the leek mixture. Add Parmesan. Stir to combine and season to taste with additional salt and pepper.

5. Warm remaining olive oil over high heat in reserved pan. When the pan is hot but not smoking, add potato mixture. Use a spatula to press mixture down into the pan firmly and evenly.

6. Turn the heat down to medium and cook potato mixture until the bottom is golden brown and potato mixture can move in the pan, about 12-15 minutes. Turn heat down to medium-low if the potatoes are browning too fast in places.

7. Place a large plate on top of potatoes and flip out of the pan.

8. Turn heat back up to high. When the pan is hot slide potatoes back into the pan and cook until the bottom is golden and cooked through, about 12-15 minutes.

9. Slide the pancake onto a serving platter, slice, and serve.

tu b'shvat apple and date salad

PARVE

A beautiful way to celebrate this under-appreciated holiday.

salad:

1   head butter lettuce torn into pieces

1   box (10 ounce) mesculin salad mix

     Seeds of 1 pomegranate (can substitute strawberries)

¼   cup pumpkin seeds, toasted

½   each unpeeled yellow, green, and red apples, cubed

8   pitted dates cut into ¼-inch rings

dressing:

2   tablespoons white wine vinegar

2   teaspoons honey

1   teaspoon Dijon mustard

1   tablespoon minced scallions, shallot, or onion

½   teaspoon kosher salt

1   clove garlic, chopped finely

     Pinch cayenne pepper

¼   cup oil

1. To prepare salad, combine salad ingredients in a bowl.

2. To prepare dressing, mix ingredients in a jar and shake well.

3. Toss salad ingredients with dressing, right before serving.

sheva minim salad

PARVE

A delicious way to enjoy all of the sheva minim of Tu B'shvat.

salad:

- 1 cup wheat berries
- ½ cup barley
- 1 cup grapes (halved if small, quartered if big)
- ½ cup dried figs (cut into small pieces)
- ½ cup pomegranate seeds
- ½ cup chopped pitted kalamata olives (optional)

honey vinaigrette:

- ¼ cup apricot jam
- ⅛ cup date honey
- 2 tablespoons vinegar
- 3 tablespoons olive oil
- 1 teaspoon salt
- ¼ teaspoon pepper

1. Boil 3 cups water. Add salt and wheat berries. Cook uncovered on low heat for about 45 minutes, or until soft. If they are ready and there is still water left, drain.

2. While wheat berries are cooking, prepare barley. In a separate pot, simmer barley in 1½ cups water about 35 minutes until soft. Drain if there is water left.

3. Put both wheat berries and barley in large mixing bowl and add the remaining sheva minim.

4. To prepare honey vinaigrette, heat jam and honey in a microwave-safe jar for 30-60 seconds until jam is melted. Remove from microwave and immediately add vinegar, then oil, and put a lid on the jar and shake until combined. Season to taste with salt and pepper.

5. Pour over salad. Mix thoroughly. Let sit at least 1 hour. Serve at room temperature.

eastern-inspired charoset

This exotic recipe is a whole new charoset experience. Enjoy!

2   pears, peeled and roughly chopped

2   Gala apples, peeled and roughly chopped

⅓   cup walnuts, toasted

⅓   cup almonds, toasted

⅓   cup pistachios, toasted

1   cup pitted dates

1   cup raisins

1   teaspoon cinnamon

½   teaspoon allspice

¼   teaspoon ground coriander

2   teaspoons grated gingerroot (optional)

1   tablespoon apple cider vinegar

1   cup sweet red wine

1. Combine fruits and nuts in food processor. Process until small clumps form, but don't purée. Add spices, vinegar and wine. Mix and refrigerate until ready to eat.

braised lamb shanks

MEAT

The perfect dish for your next Passover feast. It's easy to make with layers of complex flavors.

6 large white onions, chopped

12 lamb shanks

6 cups dry red wine

3 cups balsamic vinegar

1 cup olive oil

12 cloves garlic

6 lemons, quartered

½ tablespoon cumin

1 tablespoon coriander

6-8 large tomatoes, diced

3 tablespoons kosher salt

3 tablespoons cracked black pepper

3 bunches fresh basil, chopped

1. Preheat oven to 350 degrees.

2. Place onions in a layer in the bottom of a Dutch oven or medium roasting pan with a lid.

3. Arrange lamb shanks on top of onions. Pour wine, balsamic vinegar, and olive oil over lamb. Place a clove of garlic next to each shank, and a quarter of a lemon on each side. Add cumin, coriander, and tomatoes and season with salt, pepper and basil.

4. Cover and place in the preheated oven. Cook for 3 hours.

5. Transfer lamb shanks to a dish.

6. Purée pan juices with an immersion blender to make a sauce. Return lamb to sauce and reheat gently.

7. Alternatively, do not purée pan juices and serve shanks with gravy and onions.

trio of yom ha'azmaut dips

These recipes prove that homemade is worth the effort!

eggplant dip:

PARVE

1   large eggplant, peeled and cubed

1   tablespoon salt, plus to taste

1   medium onion, chopped

    Olive oil

2   cloves garlic, chopped

1   teaspoon dried crushed mint

    Pinch turmeric

2   tablespoons lemon juice

2   tablespoons tahini

1   tablespoon mayonnaise

1. Rinse eggplant, and salt with 1 heaping tablespoon salt. Let eggplant sit for 20 minutes, then rinse salt out.

2. Sauté onion with olive oil for about 5 minutes on medium heat, then add garlic, mint, and turmeric. Add eggplant and cover, mixing occasionally.

3. Cook for about 40 minutes until soft and mushy. Remove from heat, add salt and pepper to taste, and add lemon juice; let cool completely. When cool, add tahini and mayonnaise.

4. Refrigerate until ready to serve.

matbucha:

PARVE

1   onion, diced

    Olive oil

4   cloves garlic, diced

1   red pepper, diced

1   green pepper, diced

2-3 jalapeño peppers, diced

3   tomatoes, diced

2   tablespoons tomato paste

1   teaspoon salt

¼   teaspoon pepper

¼   teaspoon cumin

1. Sauté onion with olive oil until golden brown.

2. Add garlic and all peppers. Sauté for about 10 minutes, stirring occasionally.

3. Add tomatoes, cover pot, reduce heat to low, and cook 30 minutes, stirring occasionally.

4. Add tomato paste, salt, pepper, and cumin. Cook uncovered 10 minutes, stirring frequently to prevent burning.

hummus:

1½ cups dried chickpeas

7 large cloves garlic, unpeeled

½ cup extra-virgin olive oil, divided

¼ teaspoon ground cumin, plus more for garnish

½ cup tahini, at room temperature, divided

¼ cup plus 1 tablespoon fresh lemon juice

Salt, to taste

Paprika, for garnish

¼ cup chopped parsley

Pita bread, for serving

1. In a medium bowl, cover dried chickpeas with 2 inches water. Refrigerate chickpeas overnight. Drain chickpeas and rinse under cold water. Alternatively, bring chickpeas to a boil. Turn off heat and allow chickpeas to soak for 1 hour. Drain and rinse under cold water.

2. In a medium saucepan, cover chickpeas with 2 inches fresh water. Add garlic and bring to a boil. Simmer over moderately low heat about 40 minutes until chickpeas are tender.

3. Reserve ½ cup of cooking water and 2 tablespoons of chickpeas, then drain the rest of the cooking water. Rinse chickpeas under cold water. Peel garlic cloves.

4. In a food processor, purée chickpeas with ¼-⅓ cup of the reserved cooking water, ¼ cup of the olive oil, and 6 of the garlic cloves. Add cumin along with ¼ cup each of the tahini and lemon juice and process until creamy. Season hummus to taste with salt and transfer to a serving bowl.

5. Rinse out the food processor. Add remaining ¼ cup tahini, ¼ cup olive oil, 2 tablespoons reserved cooking water, 1 tablespoon lemon juice, and garlic clove; purée.

6. Using a ladle, make an indent in the center of the hummus. Spoon in tahini-lemon mixture. Sprinkle hummus with cumin and paprika. Garnish with the reserved whole chickpeas and parsley; serve with pita bread.

cheesecake with berry glaze

DAIRY

A gorgeous Shavuot dessert that will wow any crowd.

crust:

1   package graham crackers
2   tablespoons brown sugar
⅓   cup white sugar minus 2 tablespoons
5   tablespoons butter

cake:

1   cup sugar (¾ cup to lessen sweetness)
2   packages (8 ounce) reduced fat cream cheese
1   teaspoon vanilla extract
1   pint sour cream
3   eggs

berry glaze:

2   teaspoons cornstarch
1   teaspoon water
1   bag (12 ounce) frozen mixed berries or
      strawberries

crust:

1. Crush graham crackers. Add brown sugar with enough granulated sugar to measure ⅓ cup.

2. Melt butter and mix it with graham crackers and sugar. With your fingers, form a crust in the bottom of a foil-lined 9- or 10-inch springform pan.

cake:

1. Preheat oven to 350 degrees.

2. Cream sugar, cream cheese, and vanilla, then add sour cream. Add 1 egg at a time. Stop mixing when consistency is smooth. Pour over prepared crust.

3. Bake in preheated oven for 35 minutes. After 35 minutes, turn off the oven and allow cake to cool in oven for 1 hour without opening the oven door.

berry glaze:

1. Dissolve cornstarch in water. Add berries and bring to a boil. Pour berry glaze on top of warm cheesecake. After cake cools, refrigerate until cake is cool and topping is set.

cottage cheese cake

DAIRY

A lower fat version of the classic cheesecake that is packed with creamy deliciousness!

corn flake crust:

½   cup corn flake crumbs

¼   cup sugar

3   tablespoons butter (or margarine), softened

cake:

2   packages (8 ounce) full fat cream cheese

1⅔ cups sugar

2   teaspoons vanilla extract

16 ounces small curd cottage cheese

5   large eggs

4   tablespoons cornstarch or flour

1. To prepare corn flake crust, mix all ingredients together. Sprinkle on greased 9-inch springform pan.

2. To prepare cake, preheat oven to 350 degrees.

3. Beat cream cheese with sugar until light.

4. Add vanilla. Beat in cottage cheese along with 2 of the eggs until curds disappear.

5. Stir in remaining ingredients, one at a time, ending with cornstarch, mixing well.

6. Pour into prepared springform pan. Bake in preheated oven 1 hour until set.

7. Turn off oven and allow cake to cool in oven for several hours until room temperature.

8. Cover and refrigerate. Allow cake to stand at room temperature for at least 1 hour before serving.

Shavuot cheese blintzes

DAIRY

Making blintzes from scratch seems intimidating. This recipe makes it simple and the results are incredible!

"leaves":

3   eggs

1   cup milk

1   cup flour or whole wheat pastry flour

½   teaspoon salt

2   tablespoons sugar

cheese filling:

2   packages farmer cheese

1   egg, beaten

2   tablespoons sugar

1   teaspoon vanilla extract

⅛   teaspoon salt

     Butter or oil for frying

1. To prepare "leaves," beat first 5 ingredients together until smooth.

2. To prepare cheese filling, blend next 5 ingredients together with a fork.

3. Put a small pat of butter in a 6-inch hot skillet.

4. Pour 2½ tablespoons batter in skillet and tilt to cover surface of the pan. After a few seconds, turn and then lay on paper towel. When all the leaves are done, place the cheese mixture in the middle of each leaf, turn the sides in "envelope" style and roll.

5. Fry blintzes until crisp.

yeast-style hamentashen

If you have never tried yeast-based hamentashen, you will fall in love with this one!

dough:

1   cup sugar

¾   cup oil or margarine, melted

1½ cups orange juice

4-6 cups flour (more if needed)

1   package yeast, rapid rise or bread machine

1   teaspoon salt

3   eggs

1   teaspoon vanilla extract

poppy seed filling:

⅔   cup poppy seeds (grind well)

5   tablespoons sugar

1   tablespoon honey

    Zest of 1 lemon

1   tablespoon apricot jam (optional)

1   teaspoon cinnamon (optional)

¼   cup finely chopped raisins (optional)

1. To prepare dough, heat sugar, oil or melted margarine, and orange juice until lukewarm.

2. Place 4 cups of the flour into a mixer fitted with a flat beater or use a food processor fitted with a metal blade. Mix in yeast and salt. On low speed, add orange juice and oil mixture along with eggs and vanilla. Continue mixing until dough cleans the bowl, adding flour as needed — approximately 8-10 minutes.

3. Remove dough from mixer and transfer to a lightly floured board. Knead until dough is smooth and supple.

4. If using a food processor, pulse until a shaggy dough is formed. Remove about ½ of the dough and process remaining dough using brief pulses until dough is smooth and not sticky, adding spoonfuls of flour as needed. When dough is smooth, transfer to a lightly floured board and repeat with remaining dough. Knead dough halves together until smooth and supple.

5. Transfer dough to a lightly oiled bowl and cover. Allow dough to rise until almost doubled either overnight in the refrigerator or at room temperature for 1-2 hours.

6. To prepare poppy seed filling, mix ingredients in a medium saucepan and simmer gently for 15 minutes, stirring occasionally. Remove from heat and allow to cool. Filling may be made ahead and refrigerated, covered, for 1 week.

7. Preheat oven to 375 degrees.

8. To form hamentashen, roll a walnut-size piece of dough into a thin circle. Place a tablespoon of filling in the center and bring three sides up around the filling to form a triangle. Pinch gently to seal sides enclosing the filling. If desired, let filled hamentashen rise at room temperature for 30 minutes until puffy before baking.

9. Bake on greased cookie sheet in preheated oven for 20-30 minutes until lightly browned. Transfer baked hamentashen to a cooling rack.